Browr

352.7₄

Tempt

Brand

:creating, building and managing
brands

01/22/15

BRANDING FOR THE PUBLIC SECTOR

BRANDING FOR THE PUBLIC SECTOR

CREATING, BUILDING AND MANAGING
BRANDS PEOPLE WILL VALUE

PAUL TEMPORAL

WILEY

This edition first published 2015
© 2015 John Wiley and Sons Ltd

Registered office
John Wiley and Sons Ltd, The Atrium, Southern Gate, Chichester, West Sussex, PO19 8SQ,
United Kingdom

For details of our global editorial offices, for customer services and for information about how
to apply for permission to reuse the copyright material in this book please see our website at
www.wiley.com.

Wiley publishes in a variety of print and electronic formats and by print-on-demand. Some
material included with standard print versions of this book may not be included in e-books or
in print-on-demand. If this book refers to media such as a CD or DVD that is not included in the
version you purchased, you may download this material at http://booksupport.wiley.com. For
more information about Wiley products, visit www.wiley.com.

Designations used by companies to distinguish their products are often claimed as trademarks.
All brand names and product names used in this book and on its cover are trade names, service
marks, trademark or registered trademarks of their respective owners. The publisher and
the book are not associated with any product or vendor mentioned in this book. None of the
companies referenced within the book have endorsed the book.

Limit of Liability/Disclaimer of Warranty: While the publisher and author have used their best
efforts in preparing this book, they make no representations or warranties with the respect to
the accuracy or completeness of the contents of this book and specifically disclaim any implied
warranties of merchantability or fitness for a particular purpose. It is sold on the understanding
that the publisher is not engaged in rendering professional services and neither the publisher
nor the author shall be liable for damages arising herefrom. If professional advice or other expert
assistance is required, the services of a competent professional should be sought.

Library of Congress Cataloging-in-Publication Data

Temporal, Paul.
  Branding for the public sector : how to develop successful brands in the sector where
image is power / Dr. Paul Temporal.
     pages cm
  Includes index.
  ISBN 978-1-118-75631-7 (hardback)
   1. Government marketing.   2. Government publicity.   3. Public relations and
politics.   4. Branding (Marketing)   I. Title.
  JF1525.M37T46 2014
  352.7'48—dc23   2014022331

A catalogue record for this book is available from the British Library.

ISBN 978-1-118-75631-7 (hardback), ISBN 978-1-118-75625-6 (ebk)
ISBN 978-1-118-75627-0 (ebk)

Cover design by Wiley

Set in 10/14.5 pt PalatinoLTStd by Aptara Inc, New Delhi, India
Printed in Great Britain by TJ International Ltd, Padstow, Cornwall, UK

CONTENTS

PREFACE

This book is concerned with how the techniques of branding used so well by the world's foremost private sector companies, can and are, increasingly used by those organizations and institutions in the public sector. Public sector means nations, governments, ministries and government departments, civil services, destinations, cities, institutions, non-profit organizations, government-linked corporations and others. Branding refers to the range of strategies and techniques that create powerful identities, images, and economic wealth.

The importance of branding to the public sector is immense. Faced with the breakdown of markets and increased globalization, coupled with difficulties in securing talent, investment, government support and a competitive edge, the only path to differentiation for any public sector entity is the creation of "soft power" by creating a powerful brand strategy.

The book uses case studies and examples from governments, statutory boards, public sector ministries and departments, and other public institutions across a variety of categories and segments, and it focuses on what is happening in practice. You will find that the book covers the huge scope of the subject, from vision to valuation, and the many ways in which public sector branding can be developed and implemented with illustrations from case studies.

Although its primary purpose is not to be seen as an academic book, business faculty and students will find the techniques and cases described of great value in their studies.

Those who find themselves involved in the management of public sector organizations and branded entities will find it invaluable. If you are in charge of any aspect of public sector development, in particular policy, sector development, corporate affairs, marketing, communications, fundraising, stakeholder relationships, image building or other activities and initiatives then this book is for you.

Part One

The Importance of Branding and Building Brand Strategy

art One of this book deals with the background of why brands are important to the public sector and how strong brands are built. The first chapter gives an overview of what is meant by public sector branding, the reasons why nations and public sector organizations need to build brands, and what the resulting benefits are.

There are many forms of public sector brands and these are explored, ranging from nations and their industries, to the public service and non-profit organizations. One of the interesting features highlighted in Part One is the interaction of the public with the private sector and the effect this can have, positive or negative, on the overall nation brand. Nations and corporations can, if leveraging on each other's strengths, create a very positive Nation Brand Effect that benefits all, especially with respect to the country-of-origin concept.

Brand architecture, that is, how brands are linked together, is also explained. Although this is a private sector technique, it applies very much to the public sector too, with a strong brand architecture minimizing intra-brand competition and encouraging inclusiveness of all stakeholders in the brand-building process.

The remaining chapters in Part One focus on the techniques of building a powerful brand strategy. Prior to the creation of any strategy it is extremely important to know what the current and future desired situations for the brand are, and some consideration is given to the role and nature of market research and brand audits.

The three basic steps involved in building a brand strategy are discussed in depth, namely brand visions, brand values and personality, and brand positioning. Particular attention is given to how brands manage to create an emotional connection with their stakeholders and customers, and build this into the vision and mission; a template is provided for use in writing a brand positioning statement. Given that any brand may well be targeting groups of people who have different needs and wants, an explanation of market segmentation is provided with examples.

Once all the three steps are complete, the process moves on to brand management, communications, engagement and tracking, all of which are aspects of implementing the strategy discussed in Part Two of the book.

Chapter 1

The Public Sector and Branding

Public sector brands can be found in every country of the world, whether intentionally created or not. Public sector institutions and organizations all have relationships with individual consumers, businesses, other countries and governments, and so on, and thus they all have images of some kind. Because perceptions held by stakeholders and "customers" are so important in achieving success for the public sector, the need to control, manage and build brand images is of fundamental importance. Failure to undertake branding activity may well lead to negative perceptions and lesser achievement of national objectives.

Branding in the public sector is no longer a "nice to have" but a "must have." Increased competition in every sector makes branding an imperative. From nations to non-profit organizations, from civil services to cities, from sectors to services, there is no escape from the tough requirement of the need to create a point of differentiation and a positive image. Competition is ubiquitous and every country or public sector entity is fighting for a share of voice, talent, political support and funding. In the age of resource scarcity and constant change, the only way forward in convincing customers and stakeholders that any public sector institution or organization is different and better than others, is through the development of a strong brand. Everything else can be replicated, whether it is services, products, processes, systems, technologies or rhetoric. The only thing that any public sector entity can create that is not capable of being copied, is a powerful brand image.

Until relatively recently, branding was regarded by many as a private sector activity, and the admiration for the world's top brands has been a global phenomenon. But the public sector has now come to understand that those very same techniques that created corporate and product brands with enormous financial worth – on occasions larger than the gross domestic product of some countries – can indeed be used in exactly the same way to achieve any business or philanthropic goal.

Public sector branding is a fast-growing global trend that is here to stay. If you are in charge of any aspect of public sector development, in particular policy, sector development, corporate affairs, marketing, communications, fundraising, stakeholder relationships, image-building or other activities and initiatives, then this book is for you. You will find that the content covers the huge scope of this subject and the many ways in which public sector branding can be developed and implemented. It will also explain the globally successful techniques of branding developed by the private sector and relate these to many case examples of where the public sector has employed them.

Before I move on, let me first explain what I mean by the words "public sector." Simply put, the public sector can be defined as anything outside the private sector, but it is not quite as straightforward as that and there are some areas of overlap. The public sector can include nations or countries, public and civil service organizations, government ministries and departments, cities and other destinations, and even industries or sectors under the control of governments. In addition, there are government-linked corporations, non-profit organizations such as charities and foundations, for-profit organizations such as co-operatives, and any other non-commercial institutions or organizations such as the World Bank, NATO, or groups of countries like ASEAN (Association of Southeast Asian Nations). All of these entities can be classified under the umbrella title of "public sector." I thus take a very broad view of this area, and will give more specific examples as we move through the chapters that follow.

Why the public sector needs branding

The issue that has caused most concern in every market of the world in recent years is that of parity. Faced with a situation where their products, services, systems, processes and technology are easily replicable, the biggest challenge for corporations in the private sector has increasingly been one of differentiation. How can they appear to be different and better than their competitors when marketing and selling products and services that are so similar? The answer to this question, and the challenge, is that in the world of parity the only true differentiator is brand image. This is why people pay 1000 times the price of a Casio watch to own a Patek Philippe, and why Nike has a commanding market share of the sportswear market. It is why Louis Vuitton sales and profits continue to rise in recessionary times, and why the waiting list for luxury cars rises as prices move upwards. People are not merely buying the products associated with these examples, they are buying brands that generate emotional associations in their minds through skilful image-building techniques. They are buying for the status, prestige, self-expression and other things that they want and feel good about. The "commodity" label can be shrugged off with powerful branding. We can all give our own examples of brands we like and love from the commercial world, but what has this got to do with the public sector?

The examples from the private sector given above are all top consumer brands, but many business-to-business brands also realize the benefits, for example large companies like GE and BASF. Brands that are merely ingredients, such as Intel's branded products and other ingredient brands such as Lycra® also recognize this fact. The truth of the matter is that wherever you come into contact with a target audience that you want to influence, and whenever people are involved in an organization, institution or entity, image counts.

Let me explain more about this by giving four reasons why the public sector is now heavily involved in the world of branding, and why this activity is likely to increase in the future.

9

The first reason is that the issue of differentiation affects all organizations and institutions. For example, countries battle for tourists and foreign direct investment, and charities need to appeal for more funds. All are competing for the same target markets – in these cases, people who want to go on a vacation and those who want to be philanthropic and help the less fortunate. Just like corporations in the private sector, they have to attract various customer groups and "sell" similar products, services and ideas; just as companies have found that the best way to do this is not by lowering price, but by creating perceived value, they have to impress by building strong brand images. The perceived value of this consists not just of the tangible aspects of products and services, but also the intangible elements that exist in people's minds – how they feel and what they think about a brand. These mental associations are hugely important as they can make the difference between something ordinary and something highly sought after. Strong brands differentiate and attract people to them rather than having to chase after them. The public sector has entered the world of branding for purposes of differentiation and attraction.

A second reason for public sector interest in branding is that survival in a changing world means a demand that everyone and everything must change; relying on past reputation does not always ensure success in the future. Whatever positive brand images might have existed in the past may not remain or be desirable in the future. For example, New Zealand wants to be associated with more than just sheep and rugby, and highlights other perceptions such as a source of medical science expertise; Canada wants to be seen as a high-tech global player and world-class food producer and not just a holiday or educational destination; and Britain wants to be seen as more innovative, friendly, trendy and "with it," rather than solid, traditional, reliable and "past it." Brands need to stay relevant to consumers and keep up with change and the changing aspirations they have set themselves. The management of brand image now plays a vital role in the public sector.

Thirdly, the public sector has observed that brands are strategic assets in their own right and can bring both power and financial rewards. Some of the major rewards and benefits of branding for the public sector are outlined later in this chapter. Brands can replace the "push" factor with the "pull" factor and influence major decisions taken by large communities and groups of stakeholders in areas such as investment and funding, talent, reputation and other important variables.

Fourthly and importantly, public sector entities already have images whether they like them or not. Some of the perceptions that make up these images may be negative and some positive, but it is better to be one step ahead and manage or control these images, leveraging and strengthening the positives and playing down or removing the negatives, than allowing others to form opinions in a way that might be counterproductive.

These four reasons have led the public sector to recognize the power and rewards of branding. Just like those companies in the commercial world, the public sector has realized that greater image power means greater wealth and influence. I will discuss these benefits later and also explain how the public sector uses exactly the same techniques to build its brands as those that have proven to be so effective in the private sector.

Brands and branding

Before I summarize the chapters that follow, I would like to clarify some terminology regarding the subject of brands and branding, as these words can be misused and misunderstood.

What is a brand and what is branding?

I would like to start by saying what a brand is not. A brand is not a name, logo, a slogan, nor an advertising or public relations campaign. While these initiatives are all important in their own way and are part of a comprehensive brand building and management process, they are tactical and not strategic. They are basically communications devices that help with marketing and messaging but tend to be one way in nature, from the brand owner to the consumer. Branding happens before all of these. Secondly, a brand is not just a trademark. It is true that trademarks are a part of the management of brands as they protect them from replication and commercial fraud and form an integral part of a brand that can be reflected in monetary value.

Brands have been defined by many authors and experts in various ways, but all tend to agree that brands are a complex mixture of tangible and intangible elements. On the tangible side are products, services, communications and other "hard" aspects, while on the intangible side are "soft" aspects such as feelings, mental associations, perceptions and emotions. It is the intangible side of brands that makes them so valuable and desirable. Successful brands are emotional in nature and reflect the experiences people have with the products, services and organizations they have contact with. The simplest but most powerful definition I can offer is that brands are relationships. When a brand is being developed or managed, it is fundamentally a relationship that is being built or managed by the brand owners with current or prospective customers. This view of the brand as a relationship has particular importance for the public sector where strong relationships are critical to success. The stronger that relationship becomes, the stronger the brand will be, and this is why the experience of the customer or client at every interaction or touchpoint, is of critical importance. As with the building of any relationship, brand building is only as good as every experience encountered in that process, and this is why brand management focuses intensely on the high level of satisfaction customers or clients have across multiple touchpoints. This means that the culture of the organization has to be based on values and attitudes that reinforce what the brand stands for as it is the employees that mainly deliver the brand experience to the customer. At every level, the identity of the brand must be brought to life by those working in the organization and this is why strongly-branded companies spend a lot of time training employees to be passionately engaged with and to behave in alignment with the brand values. Developing a strong identity for the brand and bringing it to life in this way leads to success, whereas communications and other tactical activities only partially help to build brands.

The power and rewards of branding for the public sector

In the private sector, brand success can be measured in many ways but not all of these are relevant to the public sector where organizations have different, often non-commercial aims. For example, a private sector corporation may focus on brand profitability (whether for the corporation or its products), but a public sector organization may be more focused on helping to realize national objectives, however small or large a part it plays in doing this.

Looking at it from the highest level, branding can help a country to achieve its strategic objectives by clarifying what the country stands for and identifying which strategies should be used for differentiating it from other countries. Branding at a national level has led to various benefits such as:

- Increases in currency stability.
- Improvements in international credibility and investor confidence.
- Attraction of global capital.
- Increases in international political influence.
- Growth in the export of products and services.
- Increases in tourism and investment – internal and external.
- Development of stronger international partnerships.
- Enhancement of nation building (confidence, pride, harmony, ambition, national resolve).
- Attraction and retention of talent.
- Greater access to global markets.
- Reversal of negative thoughts about environmental, human rights, and other matters of importance to global audiences.
- Reversal of international ratings downgrades.

The list could go on, but these are the main, substantial benefits that governments are striving to achieve through the effectiveness and efficiency of their public sector organizations and by building strong brands.

Branding is seen in the public sector as a strategic investment that will generate strong returns and there is now a belief that when a brand is being built, it is the process of building a strategic asset with value. Not all public sector entities are aimed specifically at achieving the benefits listed previously, but by developing powerful brands, they are likely to contribute in some way towards them.

A typical example of the results and benefits gained by taking a strong branding approach at a national level is that of South Korea. Not only have they improved the value and image of their national brand, but they have ensured that government-related companies such as Samsung and others have also worked hard on their branding activities. South Korea has created a virtuous circle or link between the nation brand image and its corporate brand ambassadors, whereby if the nation brand improves, it helps the country's corporate brands; if the corporate brands do well, then this supports the country's brand image. This activity, known as the Nation Brand Effect, is led from the President's office and uses various branding techniques (see Chapter 3 for more on the Nation Brand Effect).

Moving down a level from a country to an area, England is famous for its counties with their different historic origins and distinctive dialects; destinations where there can be more than one city in each. Yorkshire is one such county in England and I have to admit to being a little biased in my choice of county for a case study, as Yorkshire is the county in which I was born.

Yorkshire is a historic county in Northern England and the largest in the United Kingdom, and is so large that for civil administrative reasons it is split up into the North, South, East and West Ridings. It has sometimes been nicknamed "God's Own Country"[1] or "God's Own County"[2] (mostly by Yorkshire people I suspect).

---

[1] https://uk.eurosport.yahoo.com/blogs/londonspy/yorkshire-10th-olympic-medal-table-135654936.html

[2] http://news.bbc.co.uk/1/hi/magazine/5234444.stm

But bias is one thing and fact is another. Yorkshire has recently won the title of Europe's Leading Destination 2013, beating Berlin, London and Madrid among other destinations. A second piece of interesting news is that Yorkshire is the first destination other than a major city or country to have won this title in the 17-year history of the award.

- An increase in the value of the visitor economy from £5.9 billion to just over £7 billion.
- Yorkshire now attracting 216 million visits per annum, the same as the Disney theme park network globally.
- Consistently being the UK's fastest-growing tourism destination, outperforming the rest of the country.
- Achieving matched funding of £36 million making the total investment in tourism promotion £76 million over the past three years.
- Procuring hard-to-achieve best value for money for the investment.
- Ensuring that Yorkshire was identified in the Government's tourism policy as one of the UK's vital "attack brands."
- Creating a smart, ambitious and confident brand which is uniting the county.
- Founding innovative ways to increase Yorkshire's visibility and profile.
- Winning the World's Best Marketing Campaign for two years running at the World Travel Awards, beating the following destinations and brands – Brazil, India, South Africa, Abu Dhabi, Qatar, Etihad Airways, Kuoni, Expedia, Visit London, Thomas Cook and Visit Scotland.
- Putting Yorkshire firmly on the UK and international map as a force to be reckoned with.

We can see from this list that there are both tangible and intangible benefits that can be earned through branding in a relatively short space of time.[3]

---

[3] www.yorkshire.com

The Welcome to Yorkshire brand intends to go further than growing the tourism economy and extend the brand to develop a stronger international profile and secure a large increase in inward investment. International network development has seen marketing activity in China, S.E. Asia India, Europe and the USA. For example, the Yorkshire messaging was seen more than 600,000 times in the back of New York cabs, and many more trade missions are planned. It intends to do this by involving both large businesses through their involvement in the Welcome to Yorkshire's Y30 group, further enhancing small business membership schemes, and involving everyone who lives and works in Yorkshire through the Yorkshire Champions scheme. An amazing aim of inclusiveness regarding Yorkshire's people is in five years' time to have every man, woman, teenager and child (post-primary school) to be able to articulate a strong message about Yorkshire and to be an active advocate. This is to ensure that the brand creates community pride so that the county speaks with one voice, as all great brands do.

The final thought I want to leave you with at this point is that public sector brands may not relate to products as they tend to do in the private sector, they are more likely to be associated with ideas, beliefs, services and causes. These are more intangible and emotional than products, and this makes branding even more important as it focuses on the building up of strong intangible thoughts, feelings and perceptions. As a result, while products and services can be replicated by other organizations, it is true to say that a brand cannot be copied and is the only thing an organization can create and offer that will provide it with a permanent source of differentiation.

The book in more detail

This book looks in considerable detail at the many kinds of public sector brands there are, how these develop or can be developed, how they can be managed, and how important they are for the countries they are in.

Part One of the book, Chapters 2 to 5 inclusive, looks at the scope and importance of branding to the public sector, and how a brand strategy is built. Part Two, Chapters 6 to 9 inclusive, looks at brand strategy implementation and management.

Using examples, Chapter 2 explores in more detail the types of public sector brands there are. Several categories of public sector brands can be found and these range from national brands to non-profit brands to individual personality brands. The concept of brand architecture is explained, with examples of how public sector brands are interrelated, and the chapter also illustrates why architecture needs to be managed to avoid unnecessary duplication of resources and intra-brand competition.

Chapter 3 looks mainly at how the combination of the private and public sector brands can make a good, or not so good, country brand. The private sector and its brands cannot be isolated from their country of origin and the public sector, and there can be a positive or negative Nation Brand Effect, depending on the relative strengths of each. This chapter also explains the concept of brand architecture and how it has implications for brand alignment, engagement, inclusiveness and intra-brand competition.

Chapter 4 moves into the field of brand strategy, answering questions concerned with how public sector brands are built using private sector techniques and some of the important issues in public sector brand development. The focus of this chapter is why brand visions and brand personalities are so important in the development of a brand strategy, and how they can create the emotional connection between a brand and its customers and stakeholders.

Chapter 5 continues looking at the elements of brand strategy and examines the role and nature of brand positioning.

The implementation and management of brand strategy is discussed in detail in Part Two of the book, which encompasses Chapters 6 to 9 inclusively.

Chapter 6 deals with the very important topic of brand management. Developing and owning a brand is one thing, but managing it and keeping it relevant is another. Brand management is a complex activity and entails not just adhering to brand strategy, but the meticulous day-to-day management of a lot of variables, some of which are not always under the control of people responsible for managing the brand. This chapter looks at the holistic nature of brand management and the activities that are necessary to ensure it is done well. Additionally, the issue of creating a brand management structure to ensure that discipline prevails and brands are kept in good condition is dealt with.

Chapter 7 examines brand communications and how both online and offline communication strategies are needed.

Chapter 8 deals with internal and external brand engagement, the importance of ensuring that all stakeholders buy-in and are aligned with the brand, and the need to build a brand culture.

In Chapter 9 the need to track brand success is explained, and by way of illustration takes a look at the ranking and valuation of nation brands, including some of the current methodology that is used by specialist valuation firms.

Finally, Chapter 10 deals with the future of public sector branding and the influences and trends that are assuming greater importance.

Throughout the book many examples are provided of various public sector brand issues and I have also included my own choice of success stories for illustration. I hope that the book provides you with some ideas on how to move forward with brand strategy, implementation and management, particularly in the public sector.

Chapter 2

Public Sector Brand Categories

The previous chapter introduced the concept of branding in the public sector, looked at the overall trend in this area, and examined some of the benefits that can be gained as a direct result of brand development and management. Now it is time to look in more depth at the types of public sector brands that exist and why the interest in branding is increasing.

Main categories of public sector brands

There are several categories of public sector brands including the following:

- multi-nation or multi-country groups
- countries or nations
- industries or sectors
- public service and civil service
- ministry and government department brands
- government-linked corporations (GLCs)
- places, destinations and cities
- non-governmental organizations (NGOs) and non-profit organizations
- personalities and leaders

Multi-national or multi-country brands

Over the past few decades there has been a trend towards countries grouping together under an "umbrella" identity or name mainly for economic purposes, and this has resulted in megabrands that include several individual country brands – brands within brands. A good example here is the European Union (EU). The EU has 28 member states or countries, but it acts as one block with respect to many legal and trade matters. When it started out as the European Economic Community (EEC) following the Treaty of Rome in the 1960s, the idea was to create a common market for the economic benefit of all European countries. As time went by, politicians cleverly expanded its role to include social issues and now the EU is getting close to managing many aspects affecting people's lives. While it does not readily admit to this intentionally, it certainly appears that it is increasingly removing individual national culture in favour of a European society. It has become a powerful brand in its own right and at one stage in the recent past, the renaming of the EU to the "United States of Europe" was considered. The head of Europe's Constitutional Convention at the time, Valéry Giscard d'Estaing, commented on the fact that the prospective change of name was in line with a re-branding of the enlarged and revamped EU. This issue remains the subject of heated debate from time to time and as an example, Viviane Reding, vice president of the European Commission and the longest-serving Brussels commissioner, called for "a true political union" to be put on the agenda for EU elections in 2014. "We need to build a United States of Europe with the Commission as government and two chambers – the European Parliament and a 'Senate' of Member States," she said.[1] Whether name changes occur, the EU has nevertheless assumed the stance of global brand, often imposing policies such as those on human rights and immigration on its sub-brands (member countries) that are a part of it.

Prestige comes with brand power and those that are not in "the EU club" are desperate to find ways of entry. It is so prestigious and offers

---

[1] Waterfield, Bruno, "We want a United States of Europe says top EU official", 8 January 2014, www.telegraph.co.uk/news/worldnews/europe/eu/10559458/We-want-a-United-States-of-Europe-says-top-EU-official.html

so many benefits that nations will alter policies, change laws, conform to social and economic conditions and even "pay" to gain entry. Individual member countries still retain their sovereignty of course, sometimes under difficult circumstances, but the EU insists on team players. Britain's obstinacy to change in certain areas, such as giving up the pound for the common euro currency, means that it is viewed as a bit of a rebel and not playing by the rules. The policy disputes between the EU and Britain are now increasing, with Britain's current government looking at a possible "stay-in/move-out" referendum to be held in 2017 (after the 2015 election), if treaty change negotiations are unsuccessful. Britain has a strong brand with its own agenda and likes to manage it in its own way and is a good example of where there can be inter-brand friction between master and sub-brands.

Other megabrands have been created through the joining of nations in pursuit of common causes, as is the case with AFTA (ASEAN Free Trade Area), the UN (United Nations), NATO (North Atlantic Treaty Organization), APEC (Asia Pacific Economic Cooperation) and ASEAN (Association of Southeast Asian Nations). ASEAN has 10 member states and it too has undergone some branding activity, with advertising campaigns promoting the ASEAN for tourism and trade in just the same way as private sector commercial brands do. It is also looking to strengthen ASEAN brand power by signing more agreements on trade between members and negotiating as one entity with other parts of the world.

By forming membership blocks like these, multi-country or multi-nation brands can gain not just economic and social benefits, but also the benefits associated with their brand images. At the time of writing, the EU brand image is somewhat tarnished with several member countries under severe financial pressure and receiving EU bailout funds in return for austerity policy changes, while the ASEAN brand is on the ascendency with member countries enjoying comparatively high growth. Economic and social factors impact on these brands just as they do with any other kind of brand.

Nation or country brands

At the next level down from multi-nation brands are the nations or countries themselves. Nation (or country) branding has been in vogue and on the increase for the last two decades, although there is some debate as to whether it is possible given its complexity. However, most people would agree that countries are trying to maximize the strong elements of their identity and image in order to be more competitive.

Several countries have acknowledged that they are undertaking some form of nation branding activities in the sense that they are not confining their activities to one industry or sector, but instead are addressing many sectors in an attempt to raise their profiles and build their images in a holistic way. Some are developed nations such as South Korea, Canada, Switzerland and Australia, and some are developing countries classified as NICs (Newly Industrialized Countries) such as South Africa, India, China, Turkey, Malaysia, Mexico and Brazil. In different ways, they are all trying to ensure that their national brands are stronger than their competitor brands. There has been considerable discussion in academic circles as to whether it is possible for a country to brand itself. The answer I give when asked this question is "Yes and No!"

Taking the "no" part of the answer first, unless a country has not existed before and is totally unknown, which is impossible, it cannot create a totally new brand, it can only attempt to influence the one it has got. Every existing country already has a brand in the form of an identity and image or images made up of various perceptions held by different people, organizations or other governments that know or have had experience of it. It is the identity (what the country wants to be seen as) and the image (how it is actually seen) that governments try to influence through branding. For example, Singapore, like many other countries I have worked in, has not systematically created a country brand image, but it does have one, undoubtedly because it possesses many images and associations held by various groups of people at home and abroad. It has a brand, but one that was not deliberately created, and there are aspects of its brand image that it would no doubt like to change. For example, although it has many brand strengths, such as efficiency, safety, reliability, confidence, good organization, cosmopolitan and more, in the past, other parts of the world have had the perception that it is also unfriendly and a little bit arrogant. It is an image that government policies are trying to change.

Sometimes, a country's image that arises from collective perceptions, can be very favourable and one that has been earned over long periods of time based on national characteristics or reputational skills; for example, Japan with consumer electronics, Germany with automotive engineering, and Switzerland with precision watchmaking. These positive images transfer on to the country image as a whole in the form of the country-of-origin effect. "Made in Germany" and "Made in Japan" bring to mind associations of high quality and innovative products.

Alternatively a country's brand images may not be desirable. Only professional market research will give a valid answer as to whether they are or are not, but if the country brand images do not match the brand identity that the country would like to project, then there will be perception gaps. For example, for many years, Canada has wanted to be seen as a high-tech player in Asia, but the reality is that it is not, despite having many strong technology companies such as Bombardier. Research shows that its image is largely confined to education and holidays. More mention will be made of what is sometimes called the Nation Brand Effect in the section discussing brand architecture in the following chapter.

To sum up so far then, the "no" answer to the original question of "Can a country brand itself?" is that a country cannot create a new brand; it can only influence what brand it has already and try to improve how it is seen in the markets it wants to be successful in. It may well have to work hard on perception management to improve its brand image.

Can countries carry out branding?

If the question "Can a country brand itself?" is changed slightly to, "Can countries carry out branding?" then the answer is a decisive "yes." Countries can and do carry out various branding activities that influence and help manage the images and perceptions that are held by various target audiences, and several countries have undergone different types of branding exercises. However, the main objectives of any national branding exercise remain the same.

The overarching goal of country branding is to find and exploit areas of strategic competitive advantage that will lead to a powerful image and the achievement of four broad objectives:

• The promotion of tourism and national culture.
• Attraction of investments and global capital.
• Increases in the exports of products and services.
• The retention and attraction of talent.

Countries are turning to branding in order to differentiate themselves from competitor nations and manage their image in order to achieve these four broad goals. They have seen that, just as in the corporate world, image power leads to economic power, wealth and success.

More than tourism is required

Traditionally, the tourism industry has been used by countries as a driver for country branding and country brand image, especially by emerging countries. In some respects, the reason for this is that it's a relatively easy market to analyse as it is well researched and also a global market.

Moreover, most countries have the basics there to satisfy the needs and wants of tourists, such as sea, sand, sun, shopping and culture.

But it is very difficult to drive a whole country brand via one industry. In tourism, for example, it is now becoming very difficult to achieve clear differentiation. If we look at a selection of slogans from a variety of countries, we see, "Amazing Thailand," "Incredible India," "It's more fun in the Philippines," and "Sparkling Korea." It is hard to make sense of these and very difficult to differentiate between them in terms of what they offer. One country that has differentiated itself quite well as a tourist destination is Malaysia, with its "Malaysia, Truly Asia" brand. With its mix of races including Malays, Chinese and Indians, Malaysia opted for a positioning designed to attract those tourists who were looking to see and engage with local culture. In spite of the fact that some "culture-seekers" will go to a country to see and experience that country's specific culture (for example, people wanting to see India's culture will go and visit that country), global research has revealed that there is a large-enough segment of people seeking culture who would visit somewhere that could offer them a variety of cultural experiences. Importantly, this choice of brand positioning fits the political agenda of the government who see the country as multi-racial and multi-cultural. Since the late 1990s, Malaysia has thus portrayed itself consistently in this way by using the brand slogan of "Malaysia, Truly Asia" and this case is described in more detail in Chapter 5 and mentioned under industry brands later in this chapter. But, however successful tourism brands are, they are not necessarily relevant to other national objectives.

There is more to country branding than tourism and thought has to be given to areas of importance such as direct foreign investment, exports, talent and other areas of importance. Tourism is a great brand builder for a country, but this and other sectors have to be brought together.

There is a downside to country branding if it happens on an industry-by-industry basis without holistic management, as a great deal of mixed messaging tends to propagate, together with a multiplicity of logos, slogans and other brand communications.

It is worth repeating that branding is not about creating logos, slogans, advertising and public relations – it is about developing competitive strategies and intentions that must not only be communicated, but also delivered on. At country level, this involves policies and public diplomacy as well as changes in behaviour across both public and private sectors. Inclusiveness is critical to success, and a failure to include all stakeholders in the branding process will almost certainly lead to intra-brand competition, a duplication of resources, and mixed messaging.

This very process creates many challenges for governments in gaining "buy-in" and commitment to brand strategies, policies and initiatives from all stakeholders, including national citizens. The size and complexity of the country branding process means that it takes time and there are no quick fixes. It is a long-term process.

It also means that there must be a firm structure to deal with all the issues that arise in the branding process – a structure that is designed both to give direction as regards brand priorities and the resources to manage the branding activities across private and public sectors. South Korea, for example, has a Presidential Brand Council that ensures the branding interface between government and industry is secured. The lesson is that country-wide brand management must not only be top-down driven but must also involve cross-sector representation. I will be discussing the notion of inclusiveness and that of structure in Chapter 6. It is tempting for governments to avoid the challenges of bringing all sectors together. Branding one or more industries can drive a country's brand image and help achieve certain national objectives where a nation feels they can generate a strategic competitive advantage. Alternatively, special attention may be given to certain strategic industries where improvements can be made that will impact on an economy and a country's image.

Industry or sector brands

Tourism has been mentioned above as the most common form of branding that countries indulge in, and most countries, large or small, do try hard to attract visitors as it is a very lucrative business and has a major impact on national prosperity. Dubai, Malaysia, South Africa, Australia, Monaco, Indonesia, Maldives, South Korea, India and many more countries have all created tourism branding strategies or at least put brand communications campaigns in place on an annual or regular basis.

Some countries have also undertaken major branding exercises for industries other than tourism. For example, Singapore has created an umbrella brand for its infocomms industry so that its many small- and medium-sized companies can gain the benefits of belonging to the strong Singapore brand as they enter into international markets; and Canada for example, has branded its agriculture and food industry. Both of these examples and others will be discussed in detail later in the book but the thoroughness of the processes in these countries aimed at global market opportunities demonstrates how seriously the subject of branding is taken. One very interesting case is that of the tiny nation of Brunei, which in order to leverage on its strengths in the halal food industry, has created an industry brand called the "Brunei Halal Brand."

CASE STUDY: The Brunei Halal Brand[2]

Brunei Darussalam is a Muslim country with a population of approximately 415 000. The first Muslim arrived in 907 and in 1368 the first Muslim ruler, Sultan Muhammad, embraced Islam. The Brunei Halal Brand is a government project initiated by the Ministry of Industry and

(continued)

---

[2] Source: *Islamic Branding and Marketing: Creating a Global Islamic Business*, Paul Temporal, 2011, John Wiley and Sons Ltd.

Primary Resources. The official website says, "Through the Brunei Halal Brand, Brunei Darussalam has set sights in becoming one of the major players of the Halal industry globally, both in terms of Halal food production and certification, with the sheer aim of catering Halal food including other Halal product of premium quality for the Muslim population worldwide."[3] The creation of the Brunei Halal Brand is in line with Brunei Darussalam's aggressive effort to move towards developing a diversified, competitive and sustainable economy. This oil-rich country has defined three sectors for development to move away from the dependence on oil and gas revenues. These are Islamic finance, Eco-tourism and Halal products.

The Halal development is the key driver of these initiatives and has three main national objectives:

- Economic diversification.
- SME (small- and medium-size enterprise) capacity building.
- Fulfilment of a "Fardhu Kifayah."

While the first two objectives might appear on many Muslim country agendas, it is the last one that perhaps sets Brunei apart. "Fardhu Kifayah" means "collective responsibility," and it is this key element that ensures the achievement of the other objectives. Undertaking the obligation of "Fardhu Kifayah" means that the acclamation to provide pure Halal food in accordance with the best Islamic standards is not just for the Brunei population, but for a wider world, and is a definite differentiator for Brunei as no other nation has declared this a priority. One of the challenges to this plan is that of the many differing Halal certification and accreditation processes that exist globally.

---

[3] www.industry.gov.bn/index.php?option=com_content&view=article&id=81&ltemid=102.

Issues in the halal certification process

There are many halal accreditation systems across the world that indicate which country or body has certified the products to be halal. For example in Brunei the label is purple with a blue background. In countries like Brunei and Malaysia it is the government that certifies the halal status, but in non-Muslim countries it may be a local mosque or organization. As there are many interpretations of Sharia law, and halal accreditation around the world is very fragmented, there is often distrust among consumers and it is unlikely that universal achievement will occur in the foreseeable future. One of Brunei's main strengths is the high standards set and arguably, its standards are becoming benchmarks for others to follow. This is seen by Brunei as a huge marketing opportunity.

Brunei considered its position and decided to create a Brunei Halal Brand that would complement its own stringent certification processes. Having seen how powerful brands can be for nations, with examples such as New Zealand lamb, Swiss chocolate, and Australian beef, Brunei decided to create a global brand itself.

The launch of the Brunei Halal Brand and its credibility

The Brunei Halal Brand was launched in 2009 to address the certification issues mentioned above and gain a sustainable competitive advantage. In the past there was real consumer concern about only meat being halal. However, consumers have an increasing awareness of all ingredients and products, showing concern over whether they are halal or not. Since detailed lists are often issued by scholars, checking every product for its halal status can be a challenging process for the average consumer. The Brunei Halal Brand is given to products considered to be of high quality and halal, and this makes it easier for consumers to select suitable products; it is its own private brand which comes with a halal certification label. This is important because consumers need to know who has certified the product as halal, and the Brunei Halal Brand clearly does that. The strictness of the standard and

(continued)

31

the tight control over the audit and certification processes by the Ministry of Religious Affairs makes the Brunei certificate more difficult to obtain than others. The advantage of gaining it is that once obtained, passing audits undertaken by other countries becomes more likely.

The process of how to build a successful international brand on this foundation was considered carefully. The high standards of halal compliance had to be matched with products of high quality, and the choice of products for particular markets correct. If a halal product is of high quality – and those are the values that Brunei Halal Brand is built on – then it is suitable for Muslims as well as non-Muslims.

Brunei runs the Halal Brand itself under its company called Wafirah Sdn. Bhd. As the company develops across the global market it also assists the SMEs by marketing their products under the Brunei Halal Brand and also by allowing them to link into a strong supply chain. By having access to this supply chain, it expands their export opportunities and creates a more competitive environment.

All companies that want to manufacture products under the Brunei Halal Brand have to pass the halal compliance audit, conducted by the Ministry of Religious Affairs Halal Food Control Division. If successful, they then have to pass audits for health and safety, plus environmental and social compliance.

A logo was developed to signify that a product had achieved Brunei Halal Brand status as well as the certification labelling. This logo was carefully chosen and is made up of three main elements:

- The diamond shape with the stylised mosque dome, representing the core Islamic values.
- The green and yellow jewel in the centre, signifying the values of the Malay Islamic Monarchy; the customs and culture of the Sultanate, and the sense of responsibility to the rainforest.
- The stylish, modern, black and white typology, in tune with today's marketplace.

With this logo as the face of the brand, Brunei values as well as products are brought into the market.

Bringing products to market

One challenge for the Brunei Halal Brand is what products to produce as taste, texture and other attributes have to be right for new products and these can vary greatly not just between countries, but even between regions within the same country. The first fifty products were unveiled on 3 June 2010 for the local market only and in particular for Ramadan, but the Brunei Halal Brand has now entered international markets, including the UK, a country with a Muslim minority.

Business opportunities

Looking forward, the target market for the brand includes the regional market, the Gulf Co-operation Council and European and American markets. Product category procurement and manufacturing opportunities will include food, pharmaceuticals, health and beauty, cosmetics, logistics and tourism. There will also be retail partnerships and investment opportunities in science, nutrition, ingredients and manufacturing. The intention is that anyone in any market that sees either Brunei's halal symbol or their certification label on a product, will automatically know that the halal compliance is of the highest standard. To bring about this global recognition is a tall order and will take some years and a great degree of financial resource to accomplish.

(continued)

Brunei is now developing a BioInnovation Corridor (BIC) to encourage investment in halal-related industry, which will also house a halal science complex.

No other country has attempted to introduce both halal certification and halal brand logos as Brunei has. Care will have to be taken to ensure that companies see the benefit of the Brunei Halal Brand in addition to the Brunei halal certification visual identity and that consumers understand the benefits of having both. It is a unique brand positioning strategy that could give a small country a large footprint on the global halal map.

There are also very significant branding opportunities for organizations within industries and sectors. For example, Brunei is aiming to use the Brunei Halal Brand to help develop its SMEs. In other industries such as education, there are both private and public sector brands existing in many countries. Sometimes they compete for investment and students, but not always, and some are funded by government and some are not. A similar situation is prevalent in the healthcare industry in many countries. In the UK, for example, the National Health Service exists alongside many private sector healthcare brands.

Public service and civil service brands

While industry branding is now becoming an accepted part of country branding, what is often neglected in country branding is the branding of the "public service," which is sometimes called the "civil service." The terminology "public service" can be defined more widely than "civil service" to include NGOs and non-profit organizations, or even government services such as the UK's National Health Service. For the purposes of this book I will use both terms to represent the civil service, which is most commonly

- The Public Service is often in the 'front line' in dealing with a country's 'customers.'
- Investors, businesses and visitors often judge a nation by the efficiency of its Public Service.
- A highly efficient Public Service can be a Brand Vector for national identity and image.
- Policies and public diplomacy influence a country's image more than trade promotions and industry, although all are important.

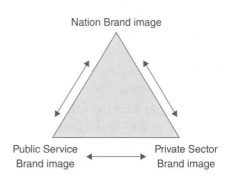

Figure 2.1 The Importance of the Public Service Brand

known as "the permanent professional branches of a state's administration, excluding military and judicial branches and elected politicians."[4]

The civil service brand image has a major impact on that of the nation, as it is the nexus between the country, its citizens, the private sector, and international relations of any kind. In any nation, the civil service is often working at the "coal face" – having multiple touchpoints with tourist, investors, companies, governments and other "customers." Figure 2.1 shows the central role played by the civil service and why it needs to become a strongly branded sector.

If a brand is a relationship, as defined in Chapter 1, then the civil service of a country will have relationships with many audiences and customers, such as current and prospective employees, parliamentarians, other governments and international organizations, citizens, and the private sector.

---

[4] www.oxforddictionaries.com

It thus comes as no surprise that a country's image depends a great deal on how efficient and effective its civil service is. A judgment on the degrees of effectiveness and efficiency on multiple dimensions can form a significant part of a country's global competitiveness ratings which are published in data sources such as the IMD World Competitiveness Yearbook. Canada's government is one that has carried out an extensive branding exercise with its public service to manage and improve its image. In 2007, the Canada Public Service Agency unveiled a major plan to brand the Public Service of Canada based on research information that revealed some gaps between the desired brand identity of the public service, and some perceptions of it held by Canadians and employees. Following the internal and external research phases, the public service brand was carefully crafted including a brand vision, mission, values, promise and character (the identity) and a positioning. All were tested via consultation with the committees and departments before the implementation framework was put in place, and the result was a solid, well-tested brand strategy that was then the subject of careful implementation activities. (This case can be read in more detail in Chapter 10.)

Ministry and government department brands

Closely connected with the public or civil service are the ministries and other government departments, or as they are jointly called in some countries such as the UK, ministerial departments. They are also highly concerned about their image and reputation as they are responsible to ministers and the government and compete with other parts of the service for talent. In most countries there are some departments that are highly desirable to work in and are perhaps seen as more "glamorous" or offering better prospects for career advancement. In Singapore, for example, many talented civil service officers would like to work for the Economic Development Board for both reasons.

Other major government organizations can be aimed at boosting the national image as well as developing infrastructure and achieving other national objectives. For example, the Qatar Foundation is one such rapidly-growing organization that could also be classified under the sections below of government-linked corporations or as a non-profit entity, and as it claims to be a non-profit entity, I have discussed this later in the chapter.

Government-linked corporations (GLCs)

Government-linked organizations or companies ostensibly work in the commercial world but are owned, part-owned or accountable to the government of a country. In Malaysia, for example, PETRONAS – the national oil company – has the freedom to work with autonomy within the commercial world, but the government has the ultimate say in what happens to the revenue PETRONAS achieves. Similarly, the Malaysian government has a "golden share" in Malaysia Airlines, the national carrier, and can impose policy or make other interventions such as board appointments and investment decisions. High-profile companies like these are important brand ambassadors to any nation and often involve themselves in brand development and management activities. Both PETRONAS and Malaysia Airlines have undergone substantial branding exercises in recent years.

Places, destinations and cities

Places, destinations and cities are commonly seen to be competing globally against other places, both for tourists and business reasons. This can be, and is referred to by some, as "Place Branding," but the terminology can sometimes be confusing, with "Place Marketing," "Destination Branding," "Destination Marketing," "City Branding" and "City Marketing" all being used by branding professionals and writers. For the sake of clarity in this book I have treated the category in the following way. My view is that destination and city brands fall under the broad category of place brands. Destination brands are normally those places that are trying to attract tourists and visitors but place brands have a wider role and can be used to attract other target audiences, such as businesses, investment and talent. Cities are both places and destinations and so fall under the place category. It could be argued that countries are places and destinations, and to some extent that is clearly true, but because of the additional complexities associated with country branding and the fact that they contain multiple places, destinations and city brands are sub-brands. The distinction between branding and marketing is that branding is the strategic foundation regarding what the brand stands for, its values and positioning; it is very inwardly focused and inclusive in its formulation with respect to stakeholders, and concentrates externally on long-term image and reputation. For example, in branding a city it is vital that local government, local businesses and the local communities are involved in the process of determining the identity of the city, how it wants to be seen, and its points of differentiation that will make it stand out from the crowd. The formulation of a brand strategy is the subject of Chapter 4. Marketing, on the other hand, is the implementation of brand strategy, is much more short term and tactical in its focus, and mainly consists of communications and engagement activities with respect to all target audiences.

Place branding has increased tremendously over the last twenty years and reflects the competition generated by the breakdown of market boundaries, speed and ease of travel and the advent of the digital world. The most well-known stand-alone city (place) brand from a communications and emotionally-driven perspective is probably New York, with the iconic and globally successful "I Love NY" campaign. The New York brand is not aligned deliberately with any USA national brand initiative but has served a dual purpose since its creation: that of acting as a city and a state brand. We will look at this from a brand strategy and a brand management perspective in Chapters 4 and 7 respectively. Yorkshire is an example of a county that has created a very good destination brand and although it has major cities existing with strong brand images such as Leeds, it has taken a broader view that has achieved a great deal of success. The Yorkshire destination brand is associated with a lot of the strong brand values linked with the UK and leverages upon these, and it has a clear set of core brand values. Brand Yorkshire and its values feature in Chapter 4 to illustrate this important point.

Liverpool is a good city brand example, perhaps not as famous as New York, but a city that has successfully built a strong brand over the last few years.

The Liverpool brand arose out of the research undertaken in preparation for its successful achievement of European Capital of Culture in 2008, by identifying the unique character that differentiated itself from other major cities in the UK. In 2008, when it held the title, over 15 million visitors (a rise of 30 per cent on 2007) brought an economic benefit of approximately £800 million. This year was a part of Liverpool's brand journey whereby over £4 billion has been spent on over 300 major developments since 2000. The heart of the brand was the Liverpool people. Indeed, the brand essence is described as "Creative Thread. Behind the familiar skyline there's a thread that runs through Liverpool past, present and future. People are the creative heart and the distinctive voice of the city."

This was further defined by the Liverpool brand personality with its warm, genuine, open, positive and energetic traits, linked to some clearly explained brand values. And in keeping with the essence, many brand ambassadors that demonstrated the city brand's values in their daily lives were appointed and used in brand communications.[5]

Destination brands are often associated with tourism and many countries are actively branding and marketing their attractions to visitors. Some of the well-known and successful branded tourism destinations include Dubai, Malaysia, and Australia.

Malaysia has been one of the most successful international tourism brands that has existed on a multi-cultural platform for over 15 years,

---

[5] www.itsliverpool.com

and has consistently communicated its central message of "Malaysia, Truly Asia" symbolizing the mix of races and associated cultures that can be seen in the country. The interesting feature of this strategy is that those people who are interested in experiencing different cultures, particularly Asian cultures, can see several in the same country without having to visit several different countries. Although there are a large number of holiday makers who wish to see a specific culture and will do so, this strategy does appeal to the remainder of the culture-seeking target audience.

But tourism is not the only sector that place brands have to bear in mind. Increasingly, place brands are competing for direct investment from companies and other organizations both inside and outside their country. Here the strategy and management of the brand has to deal with a wholly different set of questions asked by potential investors who will be looking to see if the vision for the place is a good fit for the vision of their businesses. Importantly, they will be looking at whether the right policies exist and whether the public sector leaders have the capability to deliver on the promises made.

Non-government and non-profit organizations

Moving away from direct governmental ownership in the public sector we find a variety of organizations in an interesting and fairly broad category that exists to follow certain causes, beliefs and values which are usually involved in giving aid in terms of money and service assistance to vulnerable people. They are largely philanthropic in nature and are sometimes classified as non-governmental organizations (NGOs) and non-profit organizations. These can include charities such as Oxfam and the Red Cross, cause-specific organizations such as Greenpeace, Amnesty International, and the World Wide Fund for Nature (formerly the World Wildlife Fund), foundations such as the W. K. Kellogg Foundation or The Bill & Melinda Gates Foundation, and multi-national government-linked agencies such as The United Nations Children's Fund (UNICEF). These examples are globally well-known ones but they are accompanied in this category by literally hundreds of other organizations that exist to pursue multiple and diverse philanthropic causes from alleviating poverty to assisting disabled war veterans.

Fundamentally, non-profit brands are based on integrity and ethics. The causes, beliefs and values they espouse are the foundations of their brand identities, and they attract employees and "customers" who align themselves with those core values. Internal brand engagement is very important for non-profit brands as employees that share the organization's values can be very influential in acting as brand advocates helping to build a strong culture inside, and promoting the brand outside the workplace. They rely on building trust through ethical activities related to their vision or mission and values and the integrity they exhibit both internally and externally in the way they operate, ensures the brand is managed with a high degree of focus. They are very concerned with creating and keeping strong emotional connections with people.

While profit-making companies sometimes get involved in cause-related activities under the guise of corporate social responsibility, few do this in a long-term sustainable way – exceptions being for-profit brands such as The Body Shop and Innocent Drinks, and co-operatives that are owned by customers and/or employees. Non-profit organizations are wholly committed to their cause and its associated values over the long term and believe themselves to be driven by socially responsibility. A failure to demonstrate this and adhere to their mission and values would undermine the trust element they so badly need to survive and grow.

To these non-profit organizations branding is essential, not just to get their messages out, but also to influence supporters and investors, although they tend not to get distracted by focusing on public relations and communications for fundraising alone at the expense of their image.

The larger organizations leverage on their global brand awareness and use their influence to bring about success with partnerships and international strategies. The smaller ones need to gain brand awareness and a share-of-voice in what is an extremely cluttered market, and they in particular are competing for investment without which they cannot survive or achieve their aims. Their target audiences may not be the same in many cases, but all face competition for investments and "charitable" contributions from governments and the public at large. This aim of branding as merely a means of raising funds for these organizations is nevertheless viewed more widely by non-profits as they realize that brands are strategic and can add power to employee satisfaction, culture- building, reputation and global awareness.

Even the larger, well-endowed foundations find branding to be essential. For example, Tom Scott holds the position of director of global brand and innovation at the Bill & Melinda Gates Foundation, where he "helps define and shape the foundation's identity and reputation through new communication efforts. He works to advance the programmatic goals of the foundation by using new and innovative tools to tell stories that have maximum impact. He oversees the foundation brand, leading a team across brand and insights, speechwriting, creative content and also manages the foundation's media grant making portfolio."[6] Scott's job is not about raising money as the organization has a great deal of it, but more to do with leveraging the foundation's brand and linking it to other brands that it works with, in different ways to generate greater social impact.

As mentioned earlier in this chapter, organizations such as the Qatar Foundation for Education, Science and Community Development could fall into this category. This is a private, non-profit organization that "serves the people of Qatar by supporting and operating programs in three core mission areas: education, science and research, and community

---

[6] Scott, Tom, article in the Huffington Post accessed 1 May 2013, www.huffingtonpost.com/tom-scott

development. The Foundation strives to nurture the leaders of Qatar. By example and by sharing its experience, the Foundation also contributes to human development nationally, regionally, and internationally."[7] This is a bit of a hybrid in terms of its classification as it does belong in the non-profit category according to the Foundation's description, but it is clearly linked to government, and in some instances is being used to build the global image of Qatar and is a vector for the growth of the national brand. Even though it may be privately owned, the private ownership is related to the Qatar country state and it is adopting a high global profile with sub-stantial amounts of commercial business involvement and private sector partnerships, including sponsorship of football teams such as Paris Saint-Germain FC (PSG). From a brand consistency point of view, the Qatar Foundation has an inconsistent architecture with not all brands using the Qatar brand name and the Foundation really acting as an umbrella brand. For example, under the Foundation, Qatar Education City and Qatar Science and Technology Park use the country name, as well as Sidra Medical and Research Center, Awsaj Academy, Ahli Bank, Al-Shaqab and Hamad bin Khalifa University. The Qatar Foundation is an example of how public sector brands can grow rapidly and in an ad hoc and somewhat inconsistent way in the absence of a formalized brand management structure.

Non-profit brands can be found all over the world and reflect hundreds of causes and beliefs, but sometimes the smaller ones find it difficult to build their brands as they can be overshadowed by the media reach of the larger organizations.

Personalities and leaders

You might think it strange to see this category included in public sector branding but it is of some importance. In the private sector, leaders of companies are brand ambassadors and what they say and do, and the policies and strategies they bring into play, do have an impact on the brand image of their

---

[7] www.qf.org.qa/about

companies. If they are very well-known people they will have their own personal brand image that can exert a powerful negative or positive effect on that of the corporation. It is no different in the public sector. For example, Nelson Mandela was and still can be regarded as a national icon for South Africa, and has probably done more to project a favourable image of that country than any other single person or brand initiative. He is still a famous brand name, respected and admired the world over for all that he did.

Politicians and heads of organizations can influence perceptions of their organizations, and as public sector branding is very much to do with policies and public diplomacy as opposed to commercial advertising and customer interaction, in the private sector the element of personal branding comes into play a lot more. It is inevitable in the public domain where politics often imposes itself on brands.

In addition, not only can heads of state, politicians and other officials influence the national brand as ambassadors, they are, de facto, national brand managers as they are ultimately responsible for the brands of their countries. Lee Kuan Yew, Prime Minister of Singapore for many years, played the role of both a brand visionary and a brand manager in building a highly successful national country from virtually nothing after its split from Malaysia some decades ago.

I do not intend to delve deeper into how personalities influence brands, but it is essential for any public sector brand to be managed at all levels, and the personalities of those people in senior positions will have impact on any public sector brand. Brand management will be discussed further in Chapter 6.

Summary

- This chapter has shown the wide-ranging nature of public sector brands and has demonstrated the importance to them of creating strong brand identities for various purposes.

- There are many different types of public sector brands including:
  - multi-nation or multi-country groups
  - countries or nations
  - industries or sectors
  - public service and civil service
  - ministry and government department brands
  - government-linked corporations (GLCs)
  - places, destinations and cities
  - non-governmental organizations (NGOs), non-profit organizations, and some for-profit organizations
  - personalities and leaders
- Despite the tremendous variety of public sector brands, in all categories we find examples of branding activity.
- The need for branding arises from several sources depending on the category and the situation the brand is in, but essentially all public sector brands see the need for techniques that have proved successful in the private sector in generating growth, awareness, investment, membership, funding, and differentiation.

The next chapter looks at the link between private and public sector brands, and how this can be a major contributing factor to a nation's global competitiveness and economic wealth.

Chapter 3

The Nation Brand Effect and Brand Architecture

The previous chapter examined the different types of public sector branding and the importance of branding to organizations in this sector. In this chapter I will look at the bigger picture in terms of national identity and competitiveness and the link between these and brand imagery at public and private sector levels. I will explain how the Nation Brand Effect works in creating a virtuous brand-building circle between a nation and its corporations, the need for government support; and I'll show how brand architecture plays its role in a national scenario and from a non-governmental perspective. The starting point for this discussion is the Nation Brand Effect and its link to the country-of-origin of companies and products.

The Nation Brand Effect (NBE) and Country-of-Origin (COO)

Branding certainly does not happen overnight and the larger the entity to be branded, the more likely it is to have taken a longer time to achieve any significant effect. This is particularly true of countries, most of which have a long and unique history. A country's image is built over time and in a gradual way, and is influenced by a multitude of factors such as culture, heritage, governance, politics, products, and levels of economic development. Whilst most countries possess the age factor, emerging countries tend to be ranked lower than developed economies regarding many other factors.

On the positive side, culture and heritage occupy a large piece of potential differentiation for any country if it can market these assets well. The authenticity, history, art, attractions and destinations are all opportunities for building a strong image for those countries that have these things in abundance. Developed economies have managed to do well in establishing positive consumer images here, but emerging economies are catching up quickly as global travel restrictions, leisure infrastructure and destination-marketing efforts improve.

When emerging or developing countries do not tend to perform well compared to developed economies, it is with respect to government and politics, political stability and freedom, strong human rights records, fair legal systems, and purposeful environmental initiatives, all of which help to power up strong images because they build trust. As with the success of any brand, trust is of the utmost importance. The level of economic development as revealed by infrastructure, education, healthcare, a skilled labour force, opportunities for investment and other elements similarly help strengthen national appeal. Finally, the quality of products, services and the integrity and efficiency of companies that provide these are a deciding factor in whether the country can climb the competitiveness indices and generate image appeal.

The issue for emerging countries is that they are often at a disadvantage compared to developed countries because they do not score well on many of these influential factors, and this has a major effect on perceptions of both public and private sectors. Culture and historical legacy are probably the exceptions. This interaction of public and private sector brand images via the Nation Brand Effect (NBE) is probably the most important challenge that emerging economies have to deal with. Not only does failure to score highly on these factors determine competitiveness and the reach for developed status, it damages the NBE and COO (country-of-origin) across many markets. The NBE with its combination of public and private sector brand strengths and weaknesses is a critical issue for emerging economies and is explained further below.

The COO of any brand can impact on the image of a nation. Every nation has associations in the form of perceptions held by many different groups of people and organizations it wants to influence, and the image of the country and its reputation has an effect on every sector and company within it. If the nation has a strong brand and is well-respected for certain things then it will be easier for its industries and companies to move out into international markets and succeed. This is one half of the NBE, often referred to as the country-of-origin effect (COO). However, the reverse situation can occur, where industries and organizations from a country go out into markets and are successful, and this has a positive impact on the image of the nation. When the two halves are both positive, than the NBE is fully in play and there is a virtuous circle. If either of the halves is in a negative situation then the result tends to be a negative image for all. This link, between the public sector and private sector brands and how they influence each other, is important and worthy of more explanation via some examples.

The link between private and public sector brands

Public and private sector brands have a symbiotic relationship that can work very favourably for all and again this is most evident in developed countries. For example, the United States, with its associations of freedom and success etc., has been a catalyst for the development of brands like Levi's, Nike, Timberland and others. By contrast, Coca-Cola, Apple, MTV and Intel have helped boost the image of the nation via their sheer global presence. The two-way effect is seen with Apple as an excellent example of a brand that benefits from tapping into the NBE of the USA with its award-winning "Think Different Campaign" that was cleverly attached to the US core values of independence, self-expression, freedom, creativity, etc. Quite literally, when we purchase products such as these, we are really buying a part of America and its values.

Germany is associated with precision engineering, and feeds off brands like Mercedes-Benz and BMW, just as the brands themselves do with the "Made in Germany" label. France is the home of chic with Chanel, Christian Dior, Louis Vuitton, L'Oréal and other brands.

Brands that move around the world help improve a nation's image, not to mention its "bottom line." They are national brand ambassadors. Unfortunately for some countries, their brands do not promote their COO when it would be helpful, as illustrated with the example of Canada you read about in Chapter 2, where the nation desired a brand image that was perceived as high-tech but did not promote itself as high-tech, and where its high-tech companies like Nortel and Bombardier did not promote their country-of-origin; a lose–lose situation.

Strong consumer brands can help change national images positively and overcome COO concerns. "Made in China" is a phrase viewed negatively and products bearing the phrase are avoided by global consumers; but nearly all of Nike's products are made in Asia, especially in China, and yet consumers don't worry about the quality as they trust the Nike brand. As a result of this trust, they put far less emphasis in their purchase decision-making on where the products come from. Local brands cannot command that respect. In fact, even local people look upon their national products with disdain in many emerging countries. They prefer to buy international brands from highly-respected and developed countries, despite the fact that they are normally sold at higher prices.

Companies and other brands are affected by the country brands they live within, particularly in certain categories. Italy is associated with fashion and style, and this perception has been driven by brands like Armani, Versace, Prada, and Gucci. Brands like Ferrari have also put Italy on the brand shopping list. So strong is the influence of these mental associations that some Asian brands have tried to hide their country-of-origin by using Italian sounding names, such as Giordano, the clothing retailer from Hong Kong. And BONIA describes itself as "The Italian Inspiration" but is in actual fact, a Malaysian brand linking itself via naming and slogans to the fashion country of the world. Switzerland and its watch industry is another example of national brand recognition, power and success. What we see in all the above examples is simply the power of the National Brand Effect; the essence, attributes and core values of the country of origin coming through to affect the positioning, differentiation, and brand identity of corporations. If a company's core values reflect the culture and expertise of the nation, then it should leverage this advantage as it will help build the brand more quickly.

However, negative perceptions are not so easy to change once they are deeply embedded. It took Japan nearly 30 years to change perceptions, moving from an image of a poor-quality producer and copier of other countries' products, to an image of a high-quality specialist in consumer electronics and motor vehicles. "Made in Japan" is now a mark of trust and superiority. This was not intended as a branding exercise, but as a matter of national survival. Nevertheless, it does show that when a country wishes to alter perceptions it can be done.

China now faces what Japan did earlier in history. Whilst it is true that quality in Japan was not very good in the 1960s, the quality perception for China is more fiction than fact. However, the problem for brand owners is that, right or wrong, perceptions are reality for those who possess them. Country-of-origin detracts from China's brand image as a producer of consumer goods in this way (and similarly for some of Asia's smaller developing countries), despite the fact that the perceptions may not be true. This is compounded by the fact that Chinese products are cheaply priced. This is a function of production cost and not necessarily related to quality; but in the eyes of global consumers, low price = low quality = poor brand. South Korea has followed a similar path to that of Japan. South Korean manufacturers such as Samsung, Kia and Hyundai have worked with their government and have overcome a similar quality and perception issue to that faced by China. This challenge is linked to its local branded companies and they need to push harder to achieve a positive NBE and address any negative national images. What this means in practice is that relevant and proactive government policies are necessary. Not only can policies help reinforce the public-private sector link but they are extremely influential in determining the overall image and strategic priorities of a country. In particular, the public sector has an important role in both putting forward government policies for approval by the cabinet and in implementing them. Joint efforts are necessary in the transformation from a negative to a positive NBE as Japan and South Korea have both demonstrated.

The impact of government policies

While the above examples of how national and commercial brands interact to generate the NBE, we can see that the same linkages apply to the public sector. I have mentioned earlier that fundamental government policies such as rule of law, human rights, freedom etc. have to be in place before a nation becomes really attractive as a brand, but there are also many more, less substantial customer experiences that can make a huge difference. An inefficient civil or public service will damage the brand image of the nation, for example, a visitor's experience at immigration or a foreign company faced with bribery demands can produce lasting positive or negative thoughts about the country.

Here is another example to show how policies, even apparently insignificant ones, can have a tremendous impact on a national image that gets magnified by the media. It also demonstrates the need to keep a close eye on competitors. A headline in a British newspaper recently said, "The number of Chinese visitors to France jumped by more than 23 per cent last year, new figures show, in the latest sign the country is trouncing Britain in attracting the highly-prized Asian customers."[1] Similarly, another newspaper reported how Chinese tourists spend around £7 billion annually on visits overseas, where Britain takes a mere £300 million of this. In late January 2014, the French government launched a 48-hour visa processing system, to coincide with the Chinese New Year. A British visa, on the other hand, can take up to five days, and is another example of where Britain is losing out in this market.

---

[1] Samuel, Henry, "How France is benefiting from Chinese tourists over Britain", 11 July 2013, www.telegraph.co.uk

Back in 2012, InterContinental Hotels' boss Richard Solomons said, "For tourists, if you've got to go through a hell of a performance to get a visa, you're just going to go to Continental Europe. So we've got multiple issues, and France and Germany are getting five, six or even seven times as many visitors from China as we are getting."[2] Alison Couper, global communications director at Hotels.com, said, "France's efforts to make their visa process faster than the UK's is now making it easier for the Chinese to visit. Our current visa system is persuading Chinese visitors to visit other places in Europe and it is British businesses that are ultimately losing out."[3]

This simple example illustrates how public sector branding success is inextricably linked with government policies and their implementation. Bureaucracy and red tape, the speed of decision-making, bribery and corruption can also be damaging for companies when considering where to invest. Governments must do all they can to make policies attractive in all parts of the public sector.

Another kind of policy that can assist a country to maximize the NBE is the giving of support directly to businesses for growth, development and branding by the government.

The Nation Brand Effect and government direct support for businesses

Both developed and developing economies need to work hard to enhance the NBE. This is particularly true in developing countries and countries that do not have many large international companies to act as global brand ambassadors. Unlike the USA and some of the more well-established European countries such as the UK and Germany, many countries have few multi-national brands and instead have economies that are

---

[2] Bridge, Sarah, "Intercontinental Hotels boss Richard Solomons says VAT and visa mess is robbing us of high-spending Chinese tourists", 5 August 2012, www.thisismoney.co.uk

[3] Bridge, Sarah, "La Grande Chinese Tourist Snatch: British hotels left furious as France launches fast-track visas in race to lure rich travellers", 27 January 2014, www.thisismoney.co.uk

composed almost entirely of small- and medium-sized businesses (SMEs). Many of these businesses would like to grow and be successful and are often export oriented, which helps their country brand economy, but they do not often possess the branding know-how or the budget to pursue this path.

This means that many countries have to act as a catalyst for business growth by giving support and financial incentives to help their small- and medium-sized businesses achieve all-round business capabilities including building strong brands. Two examples of a developing and a developed country illustrate the importance of this national activity. Malaysia has an SME Masterplan 2012–2020 as a part of its national vision to become a high-income, developed economy by 2020. SME's account for 99 per cent of all business establishments in the country and the aim is to increase their contribution to the GDP from 33 per cent to 41 per cent. In it, the Masterplan has identified six performance levers to help SME's achieve faster growth and overcome challenges they face, namely:

- Innovation and technology adoption
- Human capital development
- Access to financing
- Market access
- Legal and regulatory environment
- Infrastructure

The Masterplan includes a comprehensive action plan to accelerate SME growth that contains 32 initiatives across the six areas. To drive this plan forward, Malaysia has a very active and effective entity based in the Ministry of International Trade and Industry called SME Corp Malaysia, whose job it is to spur on the growth of the most promising entrepreneurs and SMEs and help create the global champions of the future by encouraging and assisting them to develop all-round business capabilities, including brand building.

Singapore has two government-linked organizations that carry out similar activities. SPRING Singapore helps entrepreneurs and local SMEs in a similar way, while IE Singapore helps the SMEs who are actively pursuing international growth and market access. Many countries now have some kind of mechanism to help their companies gain access to new markets, whether it is via grants, trade missions and promotions, subsidies or other means. SMEs are the engine of growth for all economies and they are the potentially large companies and brands of the future. This is why developing countries are focusing on the SMEs, and why many developed countries do so as well.

As the UK continues to recover from the financial crisis, it was announced in January 2014 that the government would offer support from UK Trade and Investment to 8900 mid-sized businesses with a turnover of between £25 million and £250 million. The concept that is being followed is to create a "Mittelstand," which is an army of medium-sized, export-oriented and often family-owned firms employing up to 500 employees, similar to the one that is the backbone of the German economy. When combined, the "Mittelstand" firms have a turnover of about €2 trillion, as much as the 30 largest companies listed on the DAX index. Approximately 99 per cent of all German companies fall into this category and 95 per cent are family owned. They employ 15.5 million people, yield over half the total economic output and are export-oriented. Trade minister Lord Livingston said, "Mid-sized businesses have the potential to be powerhouses for the economy." Talking about the need to create a UK equivalent to the German medium-sized exporting companies, a "Brit-elstand" he went on to say, "could generate up to £50 billion of extra value for the UK economy if they were operating at full potential" and "should be at the centre of government policy." "We need a long-term industrial policy. Germany has spent 60 years with an intense focus on being the best." The support for these companies will include "market information, translation services, trade missions and temporary office space overseas." The CBI agrees and says these companies in Britain are "the forgotten middle."[4]

---

[4] Sutherland, Ruth, "We're going to save the world through exports," Trade minister and former BT boss on mission to get firms to emulate German industrial machine, 24 January 2014, www.thisismoney.co.uk

No government can afford to ignore SMEs or fail to provide them with assistance for business capabilities and brand development. They are the future.

Governments also have industry priorities and often assist the most important sectors to develop faster. The link of companies and industries to governments is similar to the linkages between brands in major private sector corporations, and in brand lexicon this is called brand architecture.

The link between the Nation Brand Effect and public sector brand architecture

Many of the different types of public sector brands can and do link and interact together. Country brands link to multi-country brands and to their industry brands; the industries and the civil service are linked to smaller sector and department brands, and so on. The terminology for such linkages is brand architecture. Brand architecture can be thought of as an organization chart or family tree for brands, showing how they fit, or do not fit, together.

With large public or private sector brands there are usually three components – the master brand, sub-brands, and product brands. A private sector example of a master brand is Microsoft. It has sub-brands and products such as Windows 8 that link to the master brand to form Microsoft Windows 8. In cases like this there is a deliberate attempt to bring the different levels of brands together in order to leverage on each other, strengthen the master brand, and add power to the sub- and product brands by having the master brand name attached to them. There are occasions where private sector companies do not connect their brands in this way and allow products to act as stand-alone brands. They are commonly produced by very large corporations such as Unilever and Procter & Gamble who prefer to give their brands total autonomy;

although even these companies are now beginning to link their master brands to major products in order to achieve increased leverage and asset value.

An example of brand architecture at national level is shown in Figure 3.1 towards the end of the chapter, where the master brand is the nation or country itself. Every country has a brand image and as explained in Chapter 1 there is some sense in trying to influence this. Below the master brand in the diagram are the sub-brands in the form of ministries, ministerial departments and industries, and below these are "product" brands such as destinations, cities, related statutory boards and smaller departments and industry sectors.

The diagram below shows how a nation's brands could be optimally linked together. The master brand gives strategic direction and vision, often via government policies; the sub-brands, such as the nation's industries and the public (civil) service, implement the master brand policies and priorities and work hard at influencing their specific target audiences; and the product and service brands deliver their customer experiences, often influenced by the industry initiatives provided.

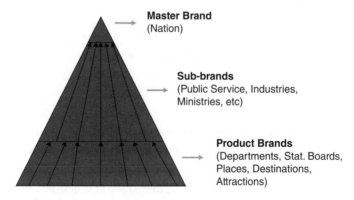

Figure 3.1 Public Sector Brand Architecture.

However, in reality, things do not usually flow so well as the national brand remains without any attempts to manage it and we thus see industry branding without a master brand, product branding not perhaps in line with government initiatives, and the public service not implementing policies either properly or at all as intended. Sometimes governments prefer to deal with branding at the mid and lower levels; thus, at a national level, if national branding is attempted, it can be extremely hard to manage and control.

Nevertheless, the important point to note here is that a change in the image of any brands or sub-brands can affect the image of the other brands with which they are associated. For example, since the financial meltdown in 2008, the banks in the UK have suffered considerable reputational damage, and this has impacted on the UK national image as a whole in a negative way, leading to economic uncertainty and contributing to ratings downgrades. The continued excessive executive payments and bonuses paid to bankers that grasped the attention of the world's media in 2012 and 2013 have also impacted negatively on the financial services industry image and that of the government as seen by citizens who perceive themselves as growing poorer and bankers getting richer.

Brand architecture and intra-brand competition

Clashes between public sector brands in the architecture pyramid can also be seen where intra-brand competition occurs. This can happen between industries and inside industries. For example, inside the tourism industry, I have mentioned above that different regions, places and destinations in a country often have different approaches to gaining visitors and directly compete in advertising and promotions. Between industries this also happens. Economic development boards send out very different messages to attract investors, and trade and industry departments have their own agendas, messages and actions. What they say and how they say it can impact on the internal and external national image. In Singapore, the three armed forces of the air force, army and navy are using a lot of resource to constantly advertise publically, even on television, in order to gain the best recruits. Thus, we often see a situation where public sector organizations compete with each other in their desire to gain more funding, better talent, the "ear" of government, and achievement of their goals.

Public sector behaviour can count in other ways too, particularly when it affects customers. For example, ministries or departments trying to attract tourism and foreign talent can be thwarted by the miserable brand experience of people entering the country through immigration or border control. Those trying to attract foreign direct investment can be neutralized by adverse foreign policy initiatives. The point I am making here is that there is usually no coherent plan to produce one consistent national brand image that addresses all audiences with one voice.

Critical to the image of any country and its desirability to attract visitors, talent, foreign direct investment and increase in trade, is the branding of the public service, and yet this is rarely seen, with government departments doing as they want and how they want within overall government policy. Many ministers have told me that often government policy is not implemented as to how they would like it to be. The public service impacts on the overall national image and the image of many sectors. One specific case study that shows some countries do take this seriously and have gone through the process of branding of the public service with specific objectives in mind, is Canada. My view is that the branding of a nation's public service will become more prevalent in the future and I have presented the Canadian public service case in Chapter 10.

Brand architecture in non-government organizations

For organizations such as non-profit and smaller brands, brand architecture is an easier process and much like private sector organizations, management and control is not as difficult as branding a large public sector entity; however, it is still essential and there can be conflicts of interest.

For instance, public sector organizations often compete with each other for talent, their reputation with the general public, and investment, but they would gain a lot more image power if they put some consistency into their brand communications.

The World Bank Group, for example, has five principal organizations:

- International Bank for Reconstruction and Development.
- International Development Association.
- International Finance Corporation.
- Multilateral Investment Guarantee Agency.
- International Centre for Settlement of Investment Disputes.

The World Bank Group allows these entities to function as stand-alone brands with different visual identities and communications strategies. None of them state the words World Bank in their titles. Arguably, the World Bank might have a lot more visibility and impact on world communities if it were to endorse these, or use another form of architectural link.

Some brands just seem to grow and grow and there is little attempt to relate the master brand to the sub-brands. I gave up trying to understand the organization chart of the United Nations, which has five "principal organs," underneath which are several funds and programmes such as UNCTAD, UNDCP, UNDP, UNEP, UNHCR, UNICEF, WFP, UNHSP, UNFPA, UNRWA; research and training institutes such as INSTRAW, UNICRI, UNITAR, UNRISD; and other UN entities like OHCHR, UNOPS, UNU, UNSSC, and UNAIDS. There are many functional commissions, regional commissions, related organizations like IAEA, WTO, OPCW, etc., specialized agencies such as ILO, WHO, FAO and lots of others as well as a huge list of secretariat bodies.

There are rumours that some parts of the UN do not even know of the existence of other parts, never mind what they do, and I would not be at all surprised. This is certainly a challenge for brand management, which, given the evident bureaucracy, is unlikely to be tackled effectively, if at all. This is another

example of intra-brand competition as many of the different sections and programmes of the UN are competing for donations from the same sources.

An example of brand architecture in a public sector non-government
organization that is beginning to gain more control of its architecture is
that of Oxfam.

CASE STUDY: Oxfam

Oxfam is a global brand that practically everyone in the world has
heard of. Physically, it is divided into Oxfam UK, where it all started,
and Oxfam International.

"Oxfam International was formed in 1995 by a group of independent non-governmental organizations. Their aim was to work together for
greater impact on the international stage to reduce poverty and injustice.

"The name 'Oxfam' comes from the Oxford Committee for Famine
Relief, founded in Britain in 1942. The group campaigned for food
supplies to be sent through an allied naval blockade to starving women
and children in enemy-occupied Greece during the Second World War.

"As well as becoming a world leader in the delivery of emergency relief,
Oxfam International implements long-term development programmes in
vulnerable communities. We are also part of a global movement, campaigning with others, for instance, to end unfair trade rules, demand better health and education services for all, and to combat climate change.

"Today, there are 17 member organizations of the Oxfam International
confederation. They are: Oxfam America, Oxfam Australia, Oxfam-in-
Belgium, Oxfam Canada, Oxfam France, Oxfam Germany, Oxfam Great
Britain, Oxfam Hong Kong, Oxfam Ireland, Oxfam India, Oxfam Inter-
món (Spain), Oxfam Italy, Oxfam Japan, Oxfam Mexico, Oxfam Novib
(The Netherlands), Oxfam New Zealand, Oxfam Quebéc."[5]

(continued)

---

[5] www.oxfam.org

Oxfam therefore, has a brand architecture that uses a shared branding approach where the master brand and sub-brands are linked which is good for consistency, although it still contains some names that do not strictly follow the rule such as Intermón. Canada is a bit odd as there is an Oxfam Canada and an Oxfam Quebéc. The difference is possibly due to the use of English and French languages, an issue that the Canadians sometimes have difficulty with.

Back in the mid-noughties the architecture was a little less neat having developed in an ad hoc way, but there seems to be a semblance of brand guardianship over the last few years to bring consistency to the core brand positioning.

Regarding positioning and communications, the look and feel of the websites are fairly consistent but the message concerning what the brand actually stands for differs slightly between countries. Although the central message is the fight against poverty, some countries add in other issues, such as women's rights (Canada) and injustice (Japan, India, America). However, as you can see from the Oxfam International website quote above, poverty is not mentioned, while a whole host of other issues are. There is always a danger that if too much autonomy is given to brands or sub-brands they may stray from the central goal, but Oxfam hasn't reached that point yet.

Private sector and public sector brands are always in danger of losing their way if they are not subject to strict discipline and management. The issue of managing brand architecture becomes even more challenging if the objective is to build a national brand. While all public sector brands have to be given a degree of autonomy at policy and communications levels, somehow at a national brand level, the performance of all brands in the public sector has to be managed. It is also extremely important to involve the private sector in the development and management of a country brand.

Some countries have tried hard to set up structures to deal with this issue and we will return to them in Chapter 6 under the heading of brand management.

Summary

- There is a strong relationship between the brand image of a nation and the corporate brands in that nation; this is called the Nation Brand Effect (NBE).
- If the national brand image is good, this helps the private sector brands to do well in international markets, and if private sector brands do well outside their country then this helps enhance the brand image of the nation. This combination will result in a strong NBE.
- If these conditions are not met, there tend to be challenges, sometimes in the form of the country-of-origin (COO) for products originating from that particular country. Similarly, corporations that do not perform well on the international stage can damage the image of their home country. The result of this lack of harmony is a weak NBE.
- Emerging or developing countries often suffer from a weak NBE as they do not score well on many factors that influence the degree of international competitiveness. This affects both the national image and the image of the countries companies and products, making it harder to do well internationally. Developed countries have stronger international competitiveness, which makes it somewhat easier to achieve a strong NBE and an effective COO effect. Any country wanting to forge a stronger NBE should provide support for its companies, especially SMEs.
- Linked to the NBE and COO effects, is the issue of brand architecture which is of extreme importance to all nations and public sector organizations. If the purpose of branding is to build up a master brand, be it a nation, an industry, the public service or even a government-linked corporation, there is a need to ensure that the sub-brands and product or service brands carry the same vision, values, and overall main message. If there is little alignment amongst all these brands then there is

likely to be intra-brand conflict, duplication of resources and expenditure, mixed messages going out in various markets, and a generally weaker master brand than there should be. This is essentially a brand management issue that is recognized and dealt with regularly, if not always well, in the private sector, but less frequently in the public sector.

- In order to solve brand management challenges there needs to be some form of brand management structure in place and brand management action plans to carry decisions through.

Chapter 6 will focus in more depth on the management of public sector brands after we have got to grips with the concept of brand strategy and how powerful brands are built, which is the subject of Chapters 4 and 5.

Chapter 4

Building a Power Public Sector Brand: Visions, Values, Emotions and Personalities

This chapter analyses and gives examples of the critical steps that have to be worked through in order to create a strong public sector brand strategy with examples from both public and private sectors. Included in brand strategy are the concepts of brand visions, brand identity, brand image, brand personality, and brand positioning, including the segmentation of target audiences. The role of market research is important and helps make the process more accurate by discovering where the brand is in terms of target audience perceptions and where it could be more advantageously changed. The techniques we refer to in building a brand strategy are those successfully used by the private sector, and that are now enthusiastically pursued by the public sector. The principles of branding are the same whatever the nature of the brand to be built and managed.

I will give a short introductory explanation of these steps before moving on to describe them in more depth with examples and cases. This chapter will focus in detail on the first two steps of developing a brand vision and personality, and Chapter 5 will explain the third step, which is developing a brand positioning.

The three main steps in building a powerful brand strategy

There are three main steps in building a brand strategy, namely the creation of:

1. An emotionally-based brand vision – this is a long-term and high-level statement (which may just be a few words) that sums up what the brand wants to stand for in the minds of consumers. A brand vision is usually emotional in nature and would be of universal appeal. The words would be relevant to the business of the brand and its potential consumer base.

2. A set of well-defined brand values, preferably (but not always) framed in the form of personality traits. Like people, brands have their own values that help in the process, allowing a brand to develop a character or personality that stands out from competitors and enables differentiation. The words that combine to form this set of values or personality link closely to the vision and when described and defined give depth and direction to brand communications and internal brand behaviour, thereby shaping the customer experience.

3. Establishing a position in the market that makes the brand stand out from its competitors. This often involves writing one or more positioning statements that bring in the competitive dimension and precisely identify why the brand is different and better than the competitor brands. Although master brand positioning statements are often general in nature and are written to describe the broad advantages of the brand they are often also written in a more tailored fashion as sub-positioning statements to focus on the differentiation for specific target audiences. They home in on who the customer is, what they are looking for in a brand, what strategic competitive advantage a brand has, and how the customer benefits from forming a relationship with the brand.

Together, these three pieces form the brand strategy and serve as a guide for employee engagement and all external brand activities. They

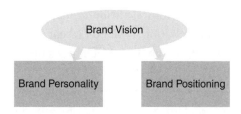

Figure 4.1 Three key components of a powerful brand strategy.

are usually given as a brief to communications, design and other agencies who may be involved in helping an organization to fully implement its brand and make the best possible impact on consumers.

Before these three main elements of brand strategy (shown in Figure 4.1) are described in detail, I would like to explain how they can be developed and influenced with accuracy and attractiveness. I will start by looking at market research as a means of discovering current perceptions and shaping the strategy using the data, and then explaining the development and role of emotion in building strong brands.

The role of market research

It is sometimes tempting to create or adjust a brand strategy based on intuition or internal consensus among a few top people but it is wise to get an outside view of a brand through market research in order to check out what others think and feel about your brand. Although some research may already be available to your organization, there is always a need to bring it up to date as market and situational dynamics change frequently, as does competitive behaviour.

Market research and brand perceptions

As a prelude to building a brand strategy, it is always preferable to find out what the present situation of a brand is and assess its key strengths and weaknesses, including any cultural attributes that may contribute towards strengthening and differentiating it. Market research can be carried out on every aspect of brand activity but the most important task is to assess what target audiences think and feel about your brand, including the people inside your organization or nation; a public sector brand is composed of both internal and external images. It is therefore important in public sector brand building to focus not only on what the desired brand identity is, but also how the reality is perceived, rightly or wrongly. This is a distinction between brand identity (how a brand wants to be seen in the marketplace) and brand image (how it is actually seen by those people that are important to its success, such as consumers, investors, analysts etc.). Whether a brand is in the private or public sector, it not only has to be good, but it has to be seen to be good. This type of consumer insight is most effective and can often reveal valuable information. The most common way of finding out about the perceptions people have about a brand is to carry out a brand audit.

Brand audits

Brand audits commonly have the following objectives in mind:

- To understand the awareness, knowledge levels, opinions and perceptions of the brand from various touchpoints based on the employees' internal brand experiences.
- To understand the perceptions of external stakeholders toward the brand and its competitors.
- To identify the gaps, opportunities and blocks in relevant areas *vis-à-vis* competition, so as to formulate a brand strategy that will resonate deeply across all key target audiences in local and international markets.
- To review the organization's vision, mission and values, and to understand the strengths and weaknesses, brand aspirations and how best to leverage on it to meet stakeholders' expectations.

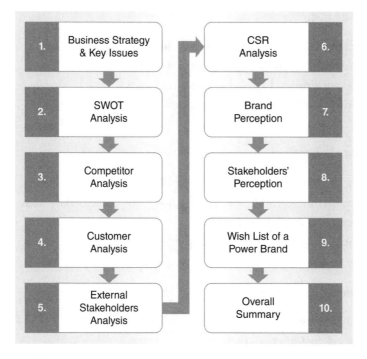

Figure 4.2 A typical brand audit.

A typical brand audit (see Figure 4.2) would cover the following sections, although the emphasis given to each may be tailored to the nature and focus of the brand and the apparent issues facing it.

The key areas for each section would include:

Business strategy and key issues:

- core business
- alignment to other entities
- growth strategy for the last five years
- growth strategy for the next five years
- current key issues
- concerns for the future
- key issues in perspective with respect to the industry or category

SWOT analysis:

- Strengths: internal and external views
- Weaknesses: internal and external views
- Opportunities: internal and external views
- Threats: internal and external views

Competitor analysis:

- local and international competitors
- competitor comparison: competitors' advantages, key areas of appeal, and weaknesses
- include internal and external perceptions

Customers:

- current customers
- target customers overall and by segment
- key consideration factors
- consideration comparison
- perceived benefits
- loyalty programmes and issues
- new products/services

External stakeholder analysis:

- current experience
- desired experience
- relationship with brand
- positive relationship
- neutral/distanced/business-like relationship
- areas of preferences
- areas for improvement
- potential relationship with brand

Corporate Social Responsibility (CSR) analysis:

- social responsibility comparison
- CSR strategy and desired end state

Brand perceptions (internal and external):

- top of mind awareness
- current brand image
- current brand personality
- desired brand image
- desired brand personality
- current brand personality comparison (internal)
- current brand personality comparison (external)

Stakeholders' (from internal and external perspective):

- customers
- public
- sponsors
- media
- strategic partners
- employees
- competitors
- government

Wish list for a power brand (internal and external):

- ideas of ways to elevate brand strength

Overall summary:

- internal perceptions: business directions and internal issues
- external environment: market and competition

- stakeholders' expectations and perception gaps
- CSR
- brand personality: current and desired

The end result of a brand audit should be a detailed roadmap of what strategic gaps exist regarding the brand in the minds of internal and external audiences. In other words, what the existing state of the organization and the brand is at this moment in time, how this compares with the desired state, and what is needed to move from the present to the existing state. Other published information can also be used to supplement that obtained from a brand audit.

Other market and competitor information

In addition to brand audits seeking information on areas such as those listed above, any public sector branding exercise needs to carry out research in all key target markets and for all industries, sectors or segments that are priorities. At a national level, several measurement or ranking systems are available for nation brands based on similar criteria, and most countries use some kind of analytical instruments to measure perceptions with target audiences and opinion makers. Some countries use global competitiveness indices such as the IMD World Competitiveness Rankings and World Economic Forum data. However, these are often supplemented with focused perception studies that are conducted in countries interested in how their brand identity and image in various dimensions compares to competitors, for example, in categories such as the ease of doing business, destination tourism, quality of living, and other areas. Also available are indices that measure national brand value such as the *BrandFinance® Nation Brands 100* index shown in Chapter 9. Some countries use a combination of all such rankings to garner as much data as possible so that they can make more informed decisions about building their public sector brands.

For example, Presence Switzerland (the legislated body responsible for the management of the Switzerland national brand) uses quantitative assessment surveys of its image in the general public of selected markets, and also qualitative interviews to find perceptions of certain themes in more depth. In addition to these, it employs permanent monitoring of both traditional leading media of important countries, especially from a foreign policy perspective, and new media such as social network sites, blogs etc. The comprehensive and regular outputs of data plus recommendations are then integrated into Switzerland's brand communications strategy in those countries via weekly, quarterly and annual reports and analyses.

Research of this nature is also important for keeping the brand fresh and relevant as the needs of people, communities, corporations and nations change over time. Hong Kong's brand was launched as BrandHK in 2001, but undertook a thorough review during 2008–2009 to co-create a shared vision for Hong Kong among local people and evaluate if the brand needed to be adjusted after its eight-year life. In this case, research was not undertaken solely on international perceptions, but a greater emphasis was placed on assessing the perceptions and aspirations of the Hong Kong community. The BrandHK Management Unit (BMU) clearly saw the need to ensure that the internal brand perceptions were as important, if not more so, than the foreign perceptions as it is difficult to build a strong external brand image if the internal brand image is weak.

The need to carry out research of this nature is not confined to national brand images, but for any substantial area under the brand, which for a nation may include industries, government-linked organizations, the public service, or other sub-brands. For example, if a tourism board wants to improve its image as a desirable destination in order to grow the number of foreign visitors, it needs to know what people think about it in major markets, as well as with respect to the major segments within those markets that it has in its sights. It needs to know what drives visitors to choose particular destinations, and how it compares to its competitors on these brand drivers.

An example of a key market and a key segment within that market would be, for example, people in the USA who intend to take a holiday in

Asia and combine it with medical treatment, which is the medical tourism segment. This is a growing segment where visitors to a country can undergo healthcare treatment such as cosmetic surgery and stay in the destination to recover with a holiday. Two competitive destinations are Thailand and Malaysia, both of which have been relatively successful in penetrating this market segment and attracting an increasing number of visitors from many countries. These countries, together with their tourism boards, have been packaging up products and services for visitors looking at this kind of vacation. Bumrungrad International Hospital in Bangkok, Thailand, is a case in point with its hybrid business model of a "Hospitel" where hospital services are centred in good locations, with service apartments where families can stay, fine dining and fast-food restaurants, hair salon and spa, and other outlets all backed up by good customer service. Understanding markets and consumers is vital for public sector as well as private sector brands, and this is another example of how the two come together in a win-win situation – the hospital with profitability and a niche market position, and the nation with a substantial number of visitors from this source.

These were the first movers into the market and they are in a good position now to catch the lucrative top end of medical tourists such as residents in the GCC (Gulf Cooperation Council) market in the Middle East, which is growing fast with a projected increase from USD 25.6 billion in 2010 to USD 43.9 billion by 2015. GCC consumers are characterized by high per capita and disposable incomes; cross-border travel is necessary for treatment as the GCC has a shortage of medical facilities including beds, staff, laboratories and clinics. Lifestyle diseases have increased rapidly with sedentary lifestyles and all six GCC countries are among the top 12 in terms of chronic diseases worldwide.[1] Niche markets exist in practically every major industry sector and can be explored on a global basis.

---

[1] AWSQ Magazine, 3 February 2014.

More examples of market segmentation will follow in this chapter under the topic of competitive positioning but for the present it is clear that research into what drives consumers to buy or invest, and how one can meet their needs and wants is vitally important.

Don't forget the competitors

Whenever market research is carried out at any level, it is critical that comparisons are made with the main competitors, otherwise the information may be very misleading. Respondents may give encouraging responses to questions about one brand but, if asked, may say even better things about an alternative competitive brand. It is absolutely crucial that the strengths and weaknesses of any brand are discovered in the research process. Without competitive comparison, any attempt to improve brand image and performance will be largely guesswork.

A market research survey that examines competitive brands on various dimensions is sometimes included in a brand audit as mentioned above. Whatever market research is commissioned, it must be remembered that it is not good enough to look at rational comparisons of data. Research concerning how people feel about a public sector brand and what they think about it are even more important, as powerful brands are developed by establishing strong emotional relationships with consumers.

The rational and emotional sides of brand strategy

We must never forget that brand promises to consumers, mainly in the media, are always made in the commercial world in terms of quality, service, and nowadays, innovation. Every organization has to be efficient and effective in what it offers to its market and this is a necessity. However, these elements are merely the price an organization has to pay to be considered by consumers and although essential, they may not be where the source of success for a brand lies. As parity becomes the norm in all these areas and brands match each other feature-by-feature and attribute-by-attribute, it is becoming harder to create a brand strategy through rational means. While consumers screen the rational elements of quality and other compelling "product" attributes as part of the buying process in order to eliminate buying options and arrive at a "short list," research tells us that the real decision to buy tends to be taken at an emotional level in a large majority of cases.

A brief excursion into medical science tells us why this is so. The notion that the rational, conscious part of the brain dominates the non-rational parts, has now been disproved. MRI scanning has revealed that people's decision-making is mostly quick and emotional, is often done subconsciously, and is much more intuitive than was previously thought. It is now widely agreed among medical experts that emotion tends to drive reason and not the other way round. Our feelings happen with great rapidity and precede conscious thought. This is mainly due to the fact that the emotional part of the brain is considerably larger than the rational part and outpaces it in terms of intensity, sending 10 times as many signals to the rational brain as opposed to the reverse. What's more, recall and memory have been proven to be a result of emotional experiences.

Neuroscience, the scientific study of the human nervous system and brain, has clarified that brand managers need to employ emotional brand strategies, as the endgame for any brand strategy is trust and loyalty, both of which are emotional in nature and not based on rational thoughts and responses. Neuroscientific techniques are increasingly being used in brand-related research by some of the top global brands, for example, to measure the intensity and longevity of human response to advertisements and product design. Given the increasing scientific evidence of the power of emotion in people's decisions and actions, we can categorically state that without emotional brand strategies it is impossible to build great brands! If we look at the powerful brands around the world, we see that they build tremendous emotional capital with their strategies and it is interesting to see what this emotional capital consists of and how they build it up.

Characteristics of power brands – emotional capital

Brand managers are increasingly turning to the emotional side of strategy in order to win and keep customers. Power brands develop emotional capital when they:

- *Are very personal:* people choose brands for very personal reasons, whether that is self-expression, a sense of belonging, or other reasons.
- *Evoke emotion:* brands sometimes unleash unstoppable emotion, arousing passion and unquestionable excitement.
- *Live and evolve:* they are like people in that they live, grow, evolve, and mature. But luckily, if they are well managed, they have no life cycle and can live forever.
- *Communicate:* strong brands listen, receive feedback, change their behaviour as they learn, and speak differently to different people depending on the situation, just as people do. They believe in dialogue, not monologue.
- *Develop immense trust:* people trust the brands they choose and often resist all substitutes.
- *Engender loyalty and friendship:* trust paves the way for long-lasting relationships and brands can be friends for life.
- *Give great experiences:* like great people, great brands are nice to be with, good to have around, and are consistent in what they give to their friends.

It is important to note that emotional capital is built up over time through becoming very close to the customer in a similar way to the closeness people have with good friends. While this is well understood and the top global corporate brands are very good at hitting most of these targets, it is not so common in the public sector and organizations need to learn more about the techniques that commercial brands use to great effect. This chapter now looks at these techniques.

Given these facts about emotional capital we need to understand that brands are really relationships, and this is the best shorthand definition to use. Whenever you are building a brand, you are building a relationship with individuals or groups of people. The founder of Starbucks, Howard Schultz, once said in a note to his employees: "I want to emphasize that the key to our success lies in our values, our culture and the relationships we have with our partners and customers. When we're at our best, we create emotional experiences for people that really enhance their lives." If this is true for all top brands – and I have no doubt about that – what is the process of establishing an emotional relationship with consumers? How do the top brands build such relationships?

The emotional brand relationship process

In order to build an emotional brand strategy there are certain steps brand managers have to take, like the steps of a ladder, as shown in Figure 4.3. Let's think of it as a relationship between two people, as opposed to a brand and consumers. For example, one person attends a function and sees someone who may be interesting to talk to; following this awareness, an opportunity to meet may arise during or after the event, and although the conversation may be short, it leads to the decision as to whether or not the interest is sufficient to carry the relationship further. Further meetings may follow and reinforce this mutual respect, and the two people then become friends. If the friendship blossoms, it generates trust and loyalty between them and it is highly likely that they will become friends for life or have a lasting relationship.

The brand–consumer relationship grows in a very similar way. Awareness comes first, followed perhaps by involvement in the form of a trial purchase or a deepening of the relationship; then a few more interactions that generate respect and a solid relationship that leads to the friendship and brand trust levels, which in turn lead to brand loyalty and lifetime customer relationships. The global power brands are very good at moving to and beyond the friendship and trust levels.

For example, in the Islamic halal food market that is worth around USD 700 billion per year, the famous global western food brand, Nestlé,

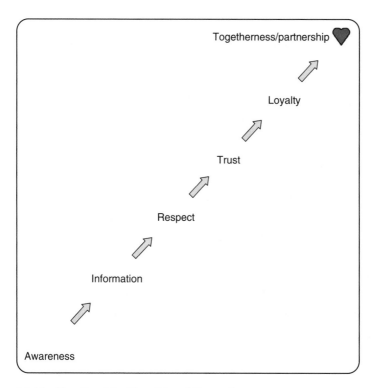

Figure 4.3 The 'Emotional Ladder of Brand Success'.

has worked with governments, state organizations and halal food experts around the world to become a major producer. With around 80 factories and a 100 product lines certified and audited by Islamic government institutions, approximately 35 per cent of the company's revenues come from halal foods. Back in 2008, the company revealed that its sales from halal foods alone stood at USD 5.2 billion. The rational element of Nestlé's success is the certification and accreditation, but the brand is globally known, admired, and trusted by people across the world. The fact that Nestlé has taken time and injected a great deal of resource into the understanding and processing of products for a huge religious market of over 1.6 billion people, has added to its trust and loyalty ratings.

The public sector has to learn from the successes of the private sector that they have to create strong relationships or they will not succeed. This is particularly important given that many public sector brands involve a high degree of service as opposed to product generation. Some public service organizations are often singled out for giving the customer poor service that influences perceptions of the national brand. Immigration and national airlines are two public sector brands that create immediate impact on brand image, as many of us can bear testament to. The brand–customer relationship is critical and this leads us to look at how emotional strategies are used to drive strong brands.

In the introduction to this chapter, I briefly explained the three main steps involved in creating a powerful brand strategy, namely the creation of a brand vision, a brand personality and a brand positioning statement. The purpose of the vision and personality is to create an emotional brand platform in terms of what the brand stands for and an identity to engage with consumers; the brand positioning statement states why the brand is different and better than other brands – a proposition. Now is the time to go into more detail with examples. The first step in creating an emotionally-driven brand strategy or relationship is to create an emotionally-driven brand vision.

Creating a brand vision

Brand visions are different from corporate visions. The latter are normally more rational in nature and tend to refer to business and market situations such as market share, return on investment and so on. Brand visions are concerned with the longer term and are largely aspirational. They define at a very top level what the brands stand for, act as a unifying factor and a source of inspiration, and drive the direction of the business and all consumer experiences. How commercial brands create emotionally-based visions is interesting and worth some elaboration, as public sector brands are now beginning to replicate this process.

Brand visions consist of a word or a few words that are of universal emotional appeal so that they can move into any market. In creating this they ensure that the emotion connects and is relevant to the business they are in. For example, we could say that the Nike brand stands for winning; an emotional attribute strongly supported by endeavour and empowerment, and that it wants to help athletes and ordinary people get the best out of themselves. The Hallmark Cards brand is focused on the business of enriching people's lives, and the brand has been quoted in the past as aspiring "to be the very best at helping people express themselves, celebrate, strengthen relationships, and enrich their lives." In expressing its beliefs the company still says, "our products and services must enrich people's lives," but its vision statement of 2014 states that, "We will be the company that creates a more emotionally connected world by making a difference to every life, everyday."[2] This is a powerful brand vision statement, and taking this view of the business has led Hallmark Cards, Inc. into a tremendous array of business opportunities across different industries and markets that have proved to be highly successful and profitable.

Can this kind of approach work for the public sector? Yes it can. Sometimes these emotional statements are called mission and not vision statements but they serve exactly the same purpose of stating exactly what the organization stands for and its purpose. For example, it certainly works for non-profit brands, such as Greenpeace International, an organization that says, "We defend the natural world and promote peace by investigating, exposing and confronting environmental abuse, and championing environmental solutions." Similarly, Friends of the Earth International has an emotional statement that says, "Our vision is of a peaceful and sustainable world based on societies living in harmony with nature." World Wide Fund For Nature (previously known as the World Wildlife Fund) says it wants to be known as, "The organization that works to stop the degradation of our planet's natural environment, and build a future in which humans live in harmony with nature." Amnesty International states that,

---

[2] http://corporate.hallmark.com/

"We are a campaigning organization; it's what we do. Our purpose is to protect people wherever justice, fairness, freedom and truth are denied." All of these statements are packed with emotional words and phrases that have universal appeal and are hard to resist, especially when aimed at people who hold similar beliefs and attitudes.

Just one word, "love," was enough to build the destination brand of New York with its "I Love NY" brand symbol and slogan. Other national or place brands such as Hong Kong SAR's BrandHK take a more rational approach; in BrandHK's case, projecting itself as "Asia's world city," could be argued as being more a positioning phrase for Hong Kong against competitors rather than a brand vision. This shorthand phrase or tagline is used in brand communications to represent what Hong Kong now stands for as distinct from what its vision of the future is. It is also a position that is close to that of Singapore, although Singapore does not actually use this phrase in its brand communications. However, Hong Kong has in the past, used a central communications message of "unlimited potential and unsurpassed opportunity," which is much more akin to an emotional view of what its present and future offer is for either business or visitors, especially when backed up by attractive and relevant creative execution.

Due to its complexity, some countries struggle with branding at national level and so settle for branding at the levels below, such as industries or sectors. As an example, Singapore has not managed to tie in all its brands under a single umbrella brand. It has struggled with this concept for many years but has been either unable, or unwilling, to attempt to bring everything together. The nearest it got to the development of an umbrella brand driven by an emotionally-driven vision was in 2010 with the formulation of the "Spirit of Singapore," but its focus was internal and based on attributes developed internally ("Nurturing," "Transforming," "Collaborating," and "Daring to Dream") intended to provide direction for all government agencies without any external usage for image projection.[3]

---

[3] Koh, Buck Song, *Brand Singapore*, Marshall Cavendish Business, 2011.

What Singapore *has* done successfully in expressing its brands externally is to focus hard on its industries, especially in the public sector. For example, Singapore branded its infocomms industry and for "Infocomm Singapore" there is a brand vision that reads, "To be the world's most trusted, intelligent and results-oriented solutions partner with the power to transform how people live, work and play."[4] This was not just a single sentence produced by a small group of people in one government department. It was derived from a substantial, inclusive, brand strategy and implementation exercise, where government agencies, small business organizations and representatives, multinational companies with a strong presence in Singapore, and successful local IT companies, all came together to create the strategy that led to successful implementation.

In Singapore's non-profit sector we can find another interesting emotionally-driven brand vision statement developed by The National Kidney Foundation Singapore (NKF), which says, "Giving life and hope through affordable, sustainable and quality renal care and education and prevention of kidney disease in partnership with the community." The focus on life, hope and partnership provides the emotional drive that has been very successful for NKF in its competition for funding and expansion.

It is clear from all these examples that the public sector is fast adopting the techniques of the global private sector brands in developing high-level brand visions that are aimed at the heart as well as the head. The use of emotion is essential for building the foundation of public sector brands.

Brand identity, brand image and perception gaps

After the establishment of a brand's vision, there needs to be a solid platform that helps that vision to be more closely defined in terms of how the brand should be seen in the marketplace. This includes brand identity,

---

[4] www.ida.gov.sg/

which are the values and/or personality of the brand – its character if you like, and the perceptions or image that the brand has. The ideal is to match the brand image with the brand identity.

Before I move on to discuss the concept of brand values and personality, I would like to emphasize the difference between the concepts of brand identity and brand image. Brand identity is how the brand wants to be seen by its target audience and is therefore internally generated by those responsible for building and managing the brand; brand image, however, is how the brand is actually seen by the people it wants to attract. This is an important distinction because if there is a difference between the two this means there are perception gaps in the market that need to be closed. Whether perception gaps exist or not is usually achieved through market research surveys and brand audits. Most market research agencies have similar proprietary instruments designed for this purpose.

Developing brand values and personality

Brand values can be both rational and emotional in nature, and many world-class power brands produce a mixture of both to capture the attention of both the left and right brains of consumers. One of the most successful ways to build an emotional brand strategy is to create a personality for your brand. The people in the real world who stand out from the crowd always seem to have some kind of "charisma." They have a personality and attitude – a character – that others respect and are sometimes in awe of. They have a presence that influences people to follow without asking and others always want to be around them. They aren't necessarily extroverted or introverted, but people feel good when they are around. Great brands are like great people in this respect, and the role of the brand manager is to manage the brand–consumer relationship by building a powerful and irresistible brand personality.

Brand values are principally derived from the vision of the brand. They are concrete words that describe what the brand stands for, its beliefs, the tone and manner in which it should speak to people, and how the brand should be managed in terms of consumer relationships. Brand values underpin the brand vision, providing a list of words that define how that vision can be translated into action.

In the commercial world, brand values are not always the same as corporate values, and personality attributes are often used to portray the brand's character. Corporate values are often very similar among companies, with words such as "teamwork" and "integrity" and "customer-focused" often being used. These kinds of values tend to set the tone of how people should behave within the organization and are used so frequently nowadays that they do not act as differentiators for organizations.

The most successful commercial brands use words that are personality-based to express their values as these are more easily transferable into action and can produce a differentiated character for the brand. They create personalities for their brands because people like people, and they think in personality terms. For example, when thinking about service standards, customers can relate to words like "friendly" more than they can to ISO 9002 or ISO 14002. If consumers experience poor service they will use terms like "unfriendly" as opposed to "poor service quality" when telling their friends about a bad brand experience. Using a personality framework to describe the brand values is therefore the best and often easiest way to attract and retain customers.

Personality characteristics such as the following have proven to be extremely attractive to most people (this is not an exhaustive list):

- caring
- modern
- innovative
- warm
- independent
- strong

- honest
- experienced
- professional
- genuine
- sophisticated
- visionary
- successful
- inspiring
- optimistic
- energetic
- trustworthy
- reliable
- approachable
- fun-loving

There are other words that could be mentioned but what is immediately noticeable is that most of these words are emotional as opposed to rational and this is because emotional brand strategies are much more successful than ones that are rationally based.

While the commercial world has learned the importance of emotionally-based brand values, the public sector is now beginning to make progress. Sometimes we can see the more corporate type of values being used, sometimes personality-type values; sometimes we see brands that have both corporate- and personality-type values in place, and some that just have the personality acting as the values. The last is an approach I use as it makes things a lot less complicated and confusing when it comes to strategy implementation.

Any public sector brand must have some core values, and nations are not exempt from this necessity. For example, the country branding of Iceland is underlined by three core values:

- *Energy:* Reflects the nature because Icelandic nature is full of green energy that can produce endless energy.

- *Freedom:* Connected to nature through its empty spaces and purity; people that are independent and a business environment that is not restricted by bureaucracy and corruption.
- *Peace:* A role in the preservation of nature and today's ecological issues. It reflects the people because they have created a safe society.

These are not the kind of values that are personality traits, but what they do have is the advantage of being defined to clearly represent their meaning. Values and personality traits are often used as the basis for brand communication.

Market research in the form of brand audits described earlier are often a good basis for seeing how a brand's values and personality are perceived and for developing the brand's character further. Decisions on which particular attributes a brand should have tend to focus on its strengths as with the Iceland example above, and these can be easily discovered by simply asking target audiences the question, "If this brand was a person, how would you describe it?" leading to some interesting findings. For example, several years ago, research was carried out on the image (perceptions) of Britain in Asia, particularly in terms of brand personality characteristics. The following personality traits were found to be predominant:

- professional
- conservative
- traditional
- well educated
- not very innovative
- likes heritage and the past
- a bit aloof
- boring (not much fun!)

The ideal personality traits desired by Britain (desired perceptions from Asian countries) at that time were:

- professional
- innovative

- dependable
- stylish

Clearly there was a perception gap here as the identity of the brand was not matched by a similar image, and the knowledge gained by this research study prompted two branding exercises that are described later in Chapter 5.

In other public sector examples connected with brand audits, Brand Hong Kong was launched in 2001 and has one set of brand values and a brand personality to accompany it. According to the BrandHK Management Unit, Hong Kong's core values are "free, enterprising, excellence, innovative and quality of living," reflecting from market research the aspirations and attitudes of its people. "Hong Kong's personality expresses its core values through its most commonly perceived attributes – cosmopolitan, dynamic, secure, diverse and connected." One could argue that these two sets of words are a little confusing as some personality characteristics (not the same ones as in the personality list) appear as core values. However, BrandHK is clearly understood internally, and externally success is there for all to see.

As all brands evolve over time and have to stay relevant to the stakeholders and potential customers, a one-year consultative review of BrandHK was undertaken in 2008–2009 using international and local research. The findings revealed that the core values and personality were still valid, but the local community had stronger aspirations for quality living and sustainable development, while innovation and creativity had become more important for Hong Kong to maintain its competitiveness as a world city in Asia. This led to some re-alignment and adjustment to BrandHK's visual identity and the revitalized BrandHK was launched in 2010.[5]

---

[5] www.brandhk.gov.hk

By contrast, Brand Australia has a clear brand personality based on the characteristics of Australians and says, "Our brand personality is a distinct part of our brand. It describes the human characteristics that we associate with our brand. These characteristics are emotionally driven and they relate to how we represent our brand to our target audience: high spirited, down-to-earth, irreverent, and welcoming."[6]

Moving on to other examples of public sector brand values, the Yorkshire brand's domestic visitor research brought out an array of attributes and personality traits, such as "natural, friendly/welcoming, peaceful, breathtaking, unspoilt, wild and rugged, relaxing, comfortable/ warm/ familiar, proud, invigorating, and enriching." Attributes that the Yorkshire brand wants to increase awareness of include, "happy/fun, exciting, and contemporary." The Yorkshire brand management team cleverly use some of these attributes to communicate different types of destinations. For example, for contemporary cities it uses exciting, contemporary and happy/fun; for seaside resorts, happy/fun, friendly, welcoming, proud and comfortable/warm/familiar. This use of leveraging different values for different purposes is a technique used a lot by the private sector when there are too many attributes to communicate in one overall, comprehensive campaign and a segmented focus is required.[7]

The City of Liverpool has a set of core values and expresses these through its brand personality. The brand values are:

- *Realness:* imaginative, dynamic, positive and productive.
- *Welcoming:* diverse, inclusive and supportive.
- *Inspirational:* exciting, thought-provoking and unique.
- *Outward looking:* open-minded, progressive and international.
- *Entrepreneurial:* pioneers, groundbreaking and experimental.

---

[6] www.tourism.australia.com/brand-australia.aspx

[7] "Understanding and communicating the Yorkshire brand", Yorkshire Tourist Board, http://webcache.googleusercontent.com/search?q=cache:http://geography.stwilfrids. com/uploads/1/2/8/9/12896421/14_yorkshire_rebranding_booklet.pdf

The core values of the city's brand are expressed through a personality and each trait is supported by a sentence similar to one that a person might actually speak. They are:

- *Genuine:* "The only front here is the waterfront. The only airs we put on are the tunes we play. Say what you mean, that's what we say."
- *Warm:* "Have you got ten minutes? Here, sit down, listen to this…"
- *Sparky:* "High energy. The streets and restaurants crackle with talk, ideas take root and grow. This is fertile ground."
- *Open:* "Tell us about where you're from. Hey, I know somebody whose cousin lives there."
- *Positive:* "Of course it can be done. You just need a bit of imagination and constructive thinking. And we've got bucket loads of that."[8]

Oxfam has quite a simple personality but it helps articulate what the brand means. It uses the words "practical visionary," and says, "It's our personality, which is at the heart of all our communications. It means that Oxfam has the vision to create major change, backed up with practical, effective solutions."[9] The World Wide Fund for Nature (WWF) is an iconic non-profit brand with a very clear set of values expressed as personality traits. WWF call this the DNA of the brand with the acronym of "KODE" and they carefully describe what the words beginning with these four letters mean.[10]

They are:

- **K**nowledgeable (science and facts-based, wise/smart, intelligent, expert)
- **O**ptimistic (Inspiring, positive, ambitious, successful)

---

[8] www.liverpoolcitybrand.co.uk/about.php

[9] www.oxfam.org.uk/what-we-do/about-us/content/new-brand

[10] www.panda.org/brandbook

- Determined (passionate, urgent, results-oriented)
- Engaging (open, available, accessible)

The WWF Brand Book goes one step further by simplifying what the characteristics mean for employee behaviour, as follows:

K – Knowledgeable

What we say and do is always based on evidence and scientific fact – though that doesn't mean we have to be dry and academic. Let's show that we understand the issues, and speak with a clear, intelligent voice.

O – Optimistic

We're all about finding solutions to some of the planet's greatest challenges. Let's get that across loud and clear by being positive and optimistic. Tell people about what we're doing to change the world.

D – Determined

We're passionate about what we do, and determined to make a difference. Let's stress the urgency of our work by showing the challenges we're tackling head-on. We don't need to scaremonger, but we do need to inspire people into action.

E – Engaging

Everything we say has to be relevant and inspiring to our audience. Let's make every message speak to as many people as we can, and convince them they need to get involved.

Defining the values in this way is really helpful in guiding and motivating everyone in the organization to adopt them and incorporate them into their everyday work.

The point to bear in mind here is that all great brands have strong values and especially a strong personality or character. Logos and slogans are not enough to explain what the brand stands for and means to internal and external audiences, but carefully explained values create consistency and inspiration for both communications and action.

As the WWF says about its brand DNA, "It's what makes us who we are. And it's there in everything that we do, from the way we decide on local policy, to how we communicate Global Initiatives. It brings coherence and clarity to our work." This holistic view of brand building is the most successful approach and in Chapter 6 it will be discussed further under the topic of brand management.

Summary

In developing any public sector brand, the process necessary to achieve success is the same as that used in the private sector. I have now described the first three steps in building a powerful brand strategy, usually preceded by a comprehensive research-based brand audit, and these are:

- Develop a brand vision that emotionally connects you with the outside world. Make this as non-limiting as possible so that the brand can appeal to many different target audiences.
- Define the brand's values in the form of personality characteristics, so that attracting and retaining customers and staff will be easier. If a brand has a set of values as well as a set of personality traits, in my experience, some confusion can arise as to why this is the situation and how and when to use the different sets.
- Visions are long term in nature, and values/personality traits do not tend to change a great deal, as is the case with the values and personalities of human beings. If brands start to make frequent changes to the visions and values and how these are expressed, then they are regarded by consumers with a degree of scepticism and even a lack of trust. People do not like to see frequent change in others, and nor

do consumers like to see frequent changes in brand messages and behaviours. People do not like unpredictable people; nor do they like unpredictable brands.

I would now like to move on in Chapter 5 to the third part of building a brand strategy, brand positioning, and this element brings in the competitive dimension. Chapters 6 through to 9 discuss the implementation of the strategy and management of the brand. In those chapters I will discuss brand communications, internal brand engagement, and intra-brand competition, as well as providing a holistic view of how a brand should be managed, its success is measured, and some challenges to look out for.

Chapter 5

Brand Positioning

The three main steps in creating a powerful brand strategy are:

- A high level, emotionally-driven brand vision.
- A set of brand values and/or brand personality attributes.
- A brand positioning statement or statements.

In the previous chapter I dealt with the first two. Once the vision of the brand is clear, and the personality (and/or core values) defined, then the other aspect that needs to be carefully considered is how to position the brand. Competitive strategy is all about being different and brand positioning has differentiation as its main objective. While brand vision and values are the long-term driving force behind this, brand positioning takes a short-term view and looks at the target market and the competitors for that market. It also has to take this shorter-term view as competitor activity and market dynamics can change on a regular basis. This includes consumer behaviour, an aspect that appears to change faster and faster each year as new technologies, products and services give the consumers more choices. Faced with a bewildering range of alternatives, the role of brand positioning is to articulate to consumers what the strategic competitive advantage of a brand is compared to other competitors and what is relevant to them. Its other primary role is to act as a guide for external brand communications, and brand positioning statements are often written as part of a brief for communications agencies.

What is brand positioning?

"Positioning" is a much-used word in the private and public sectors, and often misinterpreted. At its core, there are two questions of relevance that positioning seeks to answer, these are:

- Why is our brand different?
- Why is our brand better?

Whatever audience you wish to capture with your brand these questions have to be answered because consciously or subconsciously they are the very questions people think about when deciding which brand to choose. Later in this chapter, I will provide a template that takes a logical approach to writing a positioning statement and that can be used to answer these questions. However, firstly I wish to give a few reminders about choosing a positioning strategy for any brand.

Brand positioning considerations

When thinking about how to position a brand it is important to take into account the following:

- The position must be salient or important to the target audience you are trying to reach and influence. It is no good communicating messages to them that are of no interest or irrelevant as they will either ignore them or quickly forget them.
- The position must be based on real strengths. Making claims that cannot be substantiated can cause an enormous loss of credibility.
- The position has to reflect some form of competitive advantage. The whole point of positioning is to inform and persuade people that you are different from, and better than the competition, so whatever that point of difference is, it must be clearly expressed.

- Finally, the position must be capable of being communicated simply so that everyone gets the real intended message, and it should be aimed at motivating the audience. The aim of positioning is to provide a call to action to the target audience and to express the benefits that consumers can expect from the brand.

The need for focus

Public sector brands need to compete effectively and differentiate themselves from competitors, and this requires a good deal of focus when trying to establish strong brand positioning. In the non-profit area we can also see some good examples of focused positioning. Non-profits must answer the questions about why they are different and better, as they are competing for partners, investment, employees and a share of voice in a highly-competitive cause-related brand world. WWF is one such brand that clearly spells out the answers as shown

Positioning with Focus – The World Wide Fund for Nature (WWF)[1]

"What makes us unique? There's no other organization like WWF. These are the unique characteristics that set us apart...

"Connecting – We're a global organization: we operate across borders, environments and cultures to forge partnerships and engage individuals, communities, NGOs, corporations and governments.

(continued)

---

[1] Hudson, David and Jeffries, Barney, "One Network, One Vision, One Voice", panda.org/brandbook, ngo.media. www.ngomedia.org.uk. Concept and Design by © ArthurSteenHorneAdamson 2011. Printed by InnerWorkings. Published in February 2013 by WWF – World Wide Fund For Nature (Formerly World Wildlife Fund), Gland, Switzerland © Text 2013 WWF

"Solutions focused – We don't just identify problems: we use our unparalleled experience, our partnerships and our scientific grounding to find solutions, focusing on achievable targets, policies and results.

"Interlinked approach – We see the bigger picture: we don't look at environmental issues in isolation, but address their social, economic and political causes and effects.

"Leading – We're the world's largest membership network and have been at the forefront of conservation for half a century: we've helped bring about historic agreements and inspired millions to take action."

Having clearly-defined attributes that are factual and that can be delivered on is critical to the credibility of any brand, and WWF is a good example of this. While WWF is targeting a fairly homogenous group of people to support its activities in various ways, some other brands have to create a generic master-brand positioning and then tweak this to suit the needs of specific target audiences within the overall spectrum of consumers. This brings into play market segmentation where the needs of the different target consumers differ to some extent and have to be catered for. This is discussed later in the chapter.

Real advantages not euphoric slogans

The answer to the two questions of why the brand is different and better has to be based around one or more strategic competitive advantages the brand has and can demonstrate, and/or wish to have, and can or will make happen. This is one of the most difficult parts of the branding process, as real and significant points of difference are hard to come by. For example, if we look at tourism which is one of the largest areas of public sector branding, there are many countries that rely on slogans without any fundamental brand strengths that are really deliverable. They all claim to have sun, beaches, sand, shopping, entertainment, places of historical interest etc. to offer. So what makes the difference? Should we go to "Amazing Thailand," "Incredible India," "Jamaica – Get All Right," "Brazil Sensational," and any others that promise so much?

Consumers may become confused when they see such an array of similar slogans. The secret to having a great brand is to be able to deliver on the brand promise of the slogan or tag line that people see in the media, and some public sector brands do base their positioning on deliverables and unique points of differentiation. Continuing with the tourism theme, Malaysia is a prime example of this.

CASE STUDY: "Malaysia, Truly Asia"

The research I have carried out for some national tourism brands indicates that culture appeals to a certain segment of the global tourism market, while there are other segments interested in other things. My research showed that within the global tourism sector there is a "culture seekers" segment that is attracted to culture as a driver for choosing a particular country to visit for a holiday experience. What was interesting was that there were two sub-segments of "culture seekers." One segment was people who said that if they wanted to see and experience a certain culture they were interested in, they would only visit the country from which that culture originated. For example, if they wanted to see Indian culture they would go to India, or Chinese culture to China. However, there was another group of significance within the "culture seekers" segment that wanted to have a multi-cultural experience. So there was a position available

(continued)

to a country that could deliver on such a brand promise. Malaysia chose that route as its brand platform, and the "Malaysia, Truly Asia" brand was born.

The choice made by Malaysia was chosen to reflect not just a credible strategy for tourism growth, but a strong reinforcement of the political and social agenda concerning racial harmony. As a part of his vision for the country, former Prime Minister, Dr Mahathir Mohamad, had a central policy of racial and social harmony. The Malaysian population is composed of Malay, Chinese and Indian people in that order of dominance and who live very much as one. Even among the Malay part of the population (which is around two-thirds), there are different tribes originating from the different parts of this diverse country. The people from the Sarawak and Sabah states in the Borneo region of East Malaysia, for example, are very different to those from Kelantan in the north-east of West Malaysia, the people from Kedah near the Thai border, and the predominantly Chinese-populated island of Penang off the west coast.

For these reasons it was felt that not only could Malaysia offer the tourist glimpses of many cultures, but experience a democratic country where equality and racial harmony is practised every day. Other countries in the region have also laid claim to multiculturalism in the past, such as Indonesia, but Malaysia has maintained its position and enjoyed remarkable results with year-on-year increases in the number of visitors.

"Malaysia, Truly Asia" has never been merely a campaign, but a sustained focus for the tourism brand for over a decade, and the Malaysia Tourism Promotion Board must be credited with maintaining the consistency of its message, as opposed to many other countries that do not really create brands but tend to run a series of two- to three-year campaigns with different messages.

Nevertheless, advertising and promotional effort has been substantial and continuous with some interesting twists. For example, the Malaysian Tourist Promotion Board's (MTPB) office in the UK joined with nine tour operators in a joint advertising campaign that lasted from August 2002 to March 2003 to talk about "Malaysia, Truly Asia... Truly Affordable... Truly Breathtaking... Truly Unique Holiday Destination... and Truly Luxurious." This not only reinforced the overall brand message, but took care of other tourist concerns and wants when on holiday.

One interesting point about the branding is that the authorities haven't just confined the activities to advertising and promotion. For example, at an early stage of the brand's development, the Cultural Division of the Ministry embarked on a programme to establish cultural clubs at school level. According to then Deputy Director-General (Operations) of MTPB, Faridah Hussain, "The end result is to have Malaysians, irrespective of race, to not only appreciate each other's culture (especially performing arts) but also to perform them. This has in fact been realized in the area of music where it is common to hear (1) Malaysian melody and (2) popular songs being played by the musical groups irrespective of their racial composition." Faridah went on to say, "To my mind, the cultural groups at school level will go a long way to making performing arts more visible in this country and thus help the "Malaysia, Truly Asia" brand, which has rested on a cultural proposition."

Malaysia did not choose an easy brand proposition to differentiate itself from the other competitors, and in many ways it chose a difficult one. But "Malaysia, Truly Asia" is here to stay as the brand promise, and in the absence of prolonged competition, plus the many activities being created in the country to help make a great brand experience for visitors, more success seems likely in the future.

Malaysia has succeeded in creating a powerful and sustainable position through in-depth knowledge of the markets and the different segments that exist within them, and segmentation is explored with more examples below.

Multi-positioning and market segmentation

Market segments are parts of a market (different populations within a group) that can be served by one brand but which have different needs, wants and attitudes. For example, in the commercial world, Colgate is a brand of dental care products, but has at least 35 different product variations and formulas to suit the needs of consumers who look for different benefits of using the brand, such as whitening, total protection, sensitivity, children and others. The Colgate master brand positioning, which generically says, "We make the products that make your smile brighter and healthier!" is the main focus of consumer messaging, but many variants are targeted on the benefits that different segments are looking for.[2]

In the public sector different segments also can be seen and in some sectors such as medical tourism described earlier, spotting these can be very lucrative. Some countries have made significant progress and success with their brand development by identifying segments that only research can reveal. Tourism Australia is a good example.

CASE STUDY: Tourism Australia – Consumer Insight Research and Market Segmentation[3]

The drivers and motivators for Tourism Australia's strategy are the experiences that visitors will encounter when they visit the country. The brand proposition is, "On holiday in Australia, you don't switch

---

[2] www.colgate.co.uk

[3] This case is sourced extensively from Tourism Australia information, for example, see: *www.tourism.australia.com/markets/the-experience-seeker.aspx* accessed 3 June 2013.

off, you switch on. The unique experiences you have and the people you meet will make you feel uplifted and full of life." This is an emotional proposition and acts as a brand vision. The words "feel uplifted" and "full of life" are full of emotion and can be turned into powerful brand messages.

The key target audience is a high-yield consumer segment called, "Experience Seekers." Tourism Australia has discovered that there are common segments across different cultures that are receptive to the Australian experience, and that these Experience Seekers are likely to stay longer, spend more and travel to regional areas. They look for unique, involving and personal experiences from holidays; are informed, interested and curious about potential destinations; and tend to be long-haul travellers who do not worry too much about time, cost and distance. Travel is an important part of their lifestyle, and they are well educated and informed on many subjects. Experience Seekers cross all demographic sectors and can form up to 50% of long-haul travellers from some target markets.

Tourism Australia used demographic and psychographic research and found that Experience Seekers had the following key "wants":

- authentic personal experiences
- social interactions
- meeting and interacting with locals
- experiencing something different from their normal day-to-day life
- understanding and learning about different lifestyles and cultures
- participating in the lifestyle and experiencing it, rather than observing it
- challenging themselves – physically, emotionally and/or mentally
- visiting authentic destinations that are not necessarily part of the tourist route
- exposure to unique and compelling experiences

(continued)

Further, they were more likely to be experienced international travellers, opinion leaders, open minded and selective in their media selection. The research goes deeper than this with profiles of "Global Experience Seekers," and those in major markets such as China, Germany, Japan, USA, UK, and New Zealand. The profiles tailor the global profile and define key psychographics of the target audience in these markets.

For example, in the UK market, Experience Seekers can be self-challengers, comfort adventurers and cocoon travellers, who seek travel benefits in the form of self-esteem, accomplishment and an enriched/full life. While they have common interests in long-haul travel, for the three segments in the UK, variations occur in the travel products they actually consume to attain the Global Experience Seeker higher-level needs. In Australia Tourism Queensland identified six segments including Connectors, Social Fun-seekers, Active Explorers, Unwinders, Stylish Travellers and Self Discoverers.[4]

The research tells Tourism Australia what communication sources are likely to reach them and what products and messages are likely to attract them.

The extensive research undertaken has given rise to different campaigns and tourism Australia has five key brand messages for Experience Seekers, namely:

- Transformation: A holiday to Australia would give me a fresh perspective.
- Immersion: Holidays in Australia are about participating in life, not observing it.
- Adventure: Australia is an adventure holiday destination.
- Nature: Australia offers involving experiences in the natural environment.
- Welcoming: Australia is a welcoming holiday destination.

---

[4] http://www.parliament.qld.gov.au/documents/tableOffice/CommSubs/GreyNomad/087A.pdf

> Each of these key messages is given life by examples of what this can mean to the Experience-Seeker segments in terms of the benefits they are looking for and the products that might fulfil their needs. The brand personality for Tourism Australia ensures that the Experience Seekers receive the messages in the most appropriate tone and manner. The brand personality is emotionally driven and comprises of four characteristics, "high spirited, down-to-earth, irreverent, welcoming."

The examples above are thoroughly researched markets that lead to the discovery of opportunities for brands. Segmentation is also being used as a tool by political parties to better understand the voters.

Segmentation for political parties – voter psychographics

We have seen that it is important to fully understand current and potential customers, and governments are now looking to secure votes in democratic countries by using market segmentation techniques. In trying to understand its citizens, any government usually has a lot of demographic information concerning data such as age, income, family circumstances and other issues; but this isn't really enough to make key decisions about how to address this audience given that their feelings, attitudes, anxieties, emotions and ambitions that influence their voting intentions, may be very different. Although we know there are many people who will still vote for the same party as they always have, there are significant numbers who are more marginal and somewhat promiscuous, who see their votes as a form of self-expression and for this reason can decide election outcomes.

In countries such as the USA and the UK, government and opposition parties carry out research to understand these psychographic elements of the electorate so that they can tailor their policies, values, positioning and brand communications to them. A good example of this is the research by

Populus designed and undertaken to produce the following segmentation to profile the British electorate.

According to Populus, the psychological battleground that will determine the result of the 2015 election will be based on breaking down and addressing the British electorate into distinct clusters based on similarities in:

- Attitudes towards business and government.
- Views on inequality, immigration and social change.
- Beliefs about progress and social mobility.
- How voters assess their lives to date and future prospects for themselves and their families.

Each cluster is:

- Large enough to be statistically robust.
- Distinct enough from the other clusters to merit studying in its own right.
- Recognizable in the real world.

Mr Rick Nye, managing director of Populus says, "Populus has taken the latest profiling techniques used in the last US presidential election and now imported by the main political parties over here, and applied them to the British electorate. The result is a series of voter types based on different attitudes, outlooks and values, not just the traditional dividing lines of class or geography. These voter 'segments' as pollsters call them form the building blocks which all parties will have to try and work with to assemble the largest coalition of support they can muster at the next election."[5]

The Populus research results outlined in Figures 5.1 and 5.2 indicate the way in which the electorate voted in the last election of 2010, and the

---

[5] *A Portrait of Political Britain*, Populus, September 2013, www.populus.co.uk, reproduced with permission of Populus Limited.

The electorate, by personality type

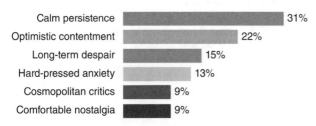

Source: *A Portrait of Political Britain*, reproduced with permission of Populus Limited

Figure 5.1 The electorate, by personality type.

profiles of people who voted for the main parties with brief descriptions are as follows:[6]

1. *Comfortable Nostalgia:* They tend to be older, more traditional voters who dislike the social and cultural changes they see as altering Britain for the worse.
2. *Optimistic Contentment:* Confident, comfortable and usually on higher incomes they are prudent and tolerant but think Britain is a soft touch.
3. *Calm Persistence:* Often coping rather than comfortable, they hope rather than expect things to get better.
4. *Hard-pressed Anxiety:* Pessimistic and insecure, these people want more help from government and resent competition for that help particularly from newcomers.
5. *Long-term Despair:* Many are serial strugglers; angry and alienated they feel little or no stake in the country or that anyone stands up for them.
6. *Cosmopolitan Critics:* Generally younger, more secular and urban-based, worried about growing inequality and the general direction the country is going in.

---

[6] *Ibid.*

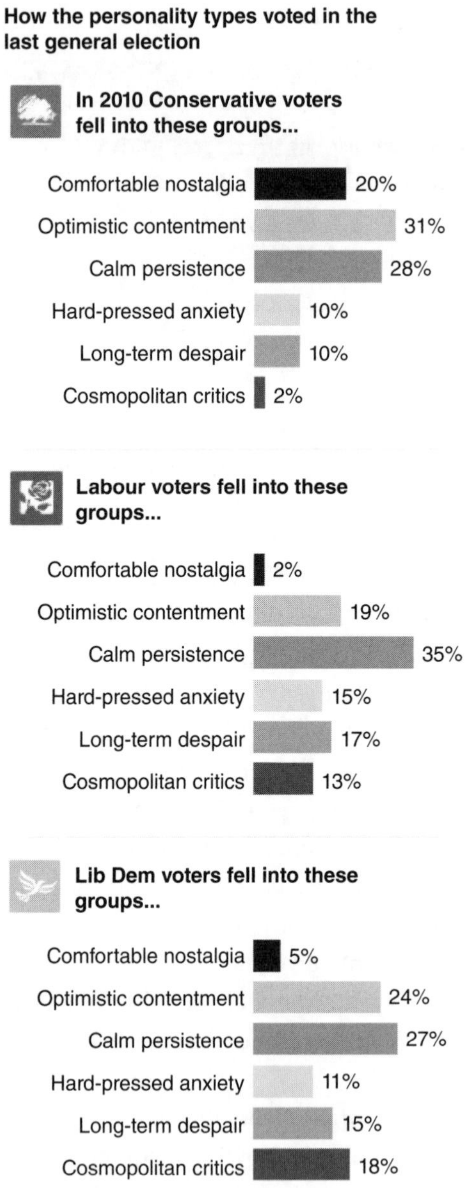

How the personality types voted in the last general election

In 2010 Conservative voters fell into these groups...

Personality type	Percentage
Comfortable nostalgia	20%
Optimistic contentment	31%
Calm persistence	28%
Hard-pressed anxiety	10%
Long-term despair	10%
Cosmopolitan critics	2%

Labour voters fell into these groups...

Personality type	Percentage
Comfortable nostalgia	2%
Optimistic contentment	19%
Calm persistence	35%
Hard-pressed anxiety	15%
Long-term despair	17%
Cosmopolitan critics	13%

Lib Dem voters fell into these groups...

Personality type	Percentage
Comfortable nostalgia	5%
Optimistic contentment	24%
Calm persistence	27%
Hard-pressed anxiety	11%
Long-term despair	15%
Cosmopolitan critics	18%

Source: *A Portrait of Political Britain,* reproduced with permission of Populus Limited

Figure 5.2 How the personality types voted in the last general election.

Similar research in the USA was carried out by the Bush and Obama presidential campaigns as explained by American author, Sasha Issenberg, who wrote in his book *The Victory Lab* about how political campaigns are now being driven less by guesswork and more by data mining such as this.

Issenberg says, "It works at the front end of the campaign and helps the politicians and their staff visualize who their voters are. It means they can craft TV ads, speeches and photo-ops that appeal to the groups they need to win over."[7]

While market segmentation works for every kind of public sector brand it does not work in certain circumstances, especially when a brand proposition is no longer effective in attracting its desired audiences. Indeed, there are occasions when research can also discover that a brand needs to reposition itself, move further away from the competition and achieve greater differentiation.

Repositioning

It is not uncommon to find that a brand needs to be repositioned. The symptoms of this can be seen in loss of investment, visitors, market share, supporters and members, and other salient aspects of the business the brand is in. There are eight reasons that are commonly found that cause the need to reposition a brand. Where there is a:

- *Poor or tarnished (outdated, not relevant any more or inconsistent) image:* for whatever reason the brand image may not be all that is desired. This is usually due to failures such as poor quality or inadequately keeping pace with changing consumer needs and wants.
- *Fuzzy or blurred image:* Sometimes the perceptions held by people are not clear; they cannot see a difference between the brand image and

---

[7] Fleming, Adam, "Take the test: Which political tribe are you?", 23 March 2014, www.bbc.co.uk/news/uk-politics-26689333

those of competitors or do not think strongly enough about it – they are indifferent. This is usually caused by unclear positioning and/or lack of good brand communications support.

- *Change in target audience or their needs and wants:* If the brand begins to focus on a new target audience it is inevitable that the positioning will need to be changed in some way to take account of the needs of the new segment. At the very least a reality check should be carried out to see whether or not a new position is needed or whether it would be too large or costly a step, perhaps even alienating existing customer groups.

- *Change in strategic direction:* Moving into completely new markets or categories may require a new positioning and this will need checking out as to acceptance of the brand and its reputation, and how this could be accomplished.

- *New or revitalized brand personality/identity:* This is the brand equivalent of cosmetic surgery. A new identity may be considered to rejuvenate the brand with a stronger and more relevant personality or set of values. Again research will be needed, and in my experience it is better for brands to go about this in an evolutionary as opposed to a revolutionary way to avoid perceptual shock and consumer disengagement.

- *Change in competitor positioning or new competitors:* Sometimes competitors can position themselves in similar ways to other brands and this may require some adjustments to positioning and communications.

- *Momentous event:* Occasionally a momentous event might occur in the form of a crisis, which may force the brand to reposition itself and change perceptions to become more favourable.

- *Re-discovery of lost values:* Sometimes when a brand has reached a point where consumers are almost taking it for granted or even beginning to move away, instead of creating a new position entirely, it might be worthwhile to revive successful brand strategies from the past and reinforce the values that have led to brand successes. Re-emphasizing heritage is one way of dealing with this issue, especially as new brands move into the market.

As competitor activity changes, so do the needs and wants of consumers. Brands therefore need to ensure that they remain fresh and relevant to address these changes. While commercial brands are somewhat easier to manage in this respect, sometimes it is not always simple and action may be too late. For example, such delayed action led to Nokia's loss of its former 40 per cent market share and its takeover by Microsoft. Moreover, it may mean radical change, as the Bentley example shows. Although owned and produced by the same companies for many decades (but not now), Bentley cars were perceived as a cheaper version of Rolls-Royce cars. This was thought to be a position that endangered sales of both vehicles, particularly Bentley. The repositioning of Bentley cars, through the creation of a sportier image supported by product development with high performance engines, moved it away from the "poor relation" perception into a powerful position as one of the world's most luxurious sports vehicles. Sales soared and it is one of the most successful repositioning stories.

For public sector brands it can be quite difficult if the brand is in bad shape or cannot easily be managed. Repositioning then, is the reversing of a brand's downward spiral of fortune by regaining a competitive advantage, or on many occasions, changing the perceptions of target audiences. Creating a new strategic competitive advantage may require attention to structural aspects of the business such as technology. Changing the perceptions of the audience may, if structurally there is nothing wrong, mean simply adjusting brand communications.

In Chapter 3 we looked at the Nation Brand Effect (NBE) and found that countries and organizations have images that contain some negative perceptions as well as positive ones. If the negative perceptions are felt to be holding back the progress of the brand, then it will be necessary to reposition the brand, in other words, change the perceptions that people have about the brand. Later on in this chapter we will look at the repositioning challenges for the UK caused by undesirable perceptions.

Repositioning and change

Repositioning is becoming more frequent as organizations seek to keep up with the pace of change and innovation. As constant innovation becomes mandatory for success, so repositioning follows in an equally mandatory manner and becomes the norm rather than the exception, taking place on a much more frequent basis. This means that brand managers have to take a different view of how they sustain and improve their market leadership and/or ambitions.

Factors to consider in repositioning brands in the world of change are as follows:

- Accept that repositioning is an essential part of brand development.
- Ensure you don't alter the personality of your product/service/company, as this will place your brand in the "unpredictable" category.
- Gather market intelligence on what the changing needs of your customers are, and the competitive response.
- Remember that you are dealing in the management of perceptions, and this means that you must budget for it. Repositioning means cash outflow in brand communications to change perceptions and make people *think* you are still, or are now, different and better. The more entrenched the unwanted perceptions are, the more you will have to spend.
- Bear in mind that all the products/services a brand has in the pipeline have to be changed according to new positioning; if this is difficult, then repositioning may encounter problems. In the case of major government policies for instance, this can take up to several years as products and services, sometimes including infrastructure developments that are in the pipeline, will slow down major repositioning.
- Get buy-in from everyone that can make an impact on the brand or the repositioning effort won't work effectively.
- Remember the basics: in order to reposition, you either have to add more value to the brand proposition, or change the target audience.

Repositioning a national or public sector brand and changing deeply entrenched perceptions is not an easy task but it can be done. Britain is a case in point, and I have been involved in two projects aimed at repositioning Britain in Asia, described below. But before I present this, I would like to suggest a framework or template that I have found works well when helping many types of public sector brands think through what their brand's positioning should be.

Writing a positioning statement

Positioning statements are internal documents and not meant for public consumption. They summarize a brand's competitive advantage and act as a guide for strategic marketing and brand management. They state specifically and briefly how any public sector organization or nation, or industry wants to be perceived. They not only spell out the desired image a brand wishes to have, but are also a good test for strategy as they have to express whether the perceptions required are believable, credible, and achievable. Positioning statements aren't easy to write and often need several drafts before a final output can be used. It is best to write them with inputs and agreement from other people. For instance, in the private sector, a positioning statement would need to be considered by as many senior managers as possible to gain consensus agreement and buy-in, and to ensure consistency of execution. Product managers would also need to seek other opinions and endorsements. In the public sector, inclusivity also has to be a part of the process and all stakeholders should be consulted in the writing of positioning statements.

Before writing a positioning statement, it is vital that there is a complete understanding of the following areas:

- *Your brand:* This seems obvious, but you have to be very clear about what your brand really stands for and is offering that will attract the people you are trying to influence. For example, for investments and destinations this will mean looking closely at all the features, attributes and benefits that people will derive from them. You should be looking for factors all the time that will help differentiate what *you* have to offer from what the competition are offering. The same goes for services. What service standards can you present that will give you the opportunity to suggest a competitive advantage? Non-profit organizations and industries themselves often have distinguishing characteristics, such as global stature, track record, personality, and other unique features that can be highlighted and used as differentiators.

- *The target audience(s) you want to influence with your brand:* Knowing what people need and want is critical, and there is a difference between the two. I might *need* some food to eat, but what I *want* is a curry. More than that, I might want a *vegetarian* curry because that kind of food fits in with my belief structure. It becomes important, therefore, to understand people's intangible requirements as well as their more tangible ones. Unless there is precision in customer understanding, the messages we send may be irrelevant and lose us credibility. The examples of Malaysia and Australia given earlier in this chapter are typical of well-researched consumer insight.
- *The competitors your brand is facing (competitive set):* No strategy is complete without a thorough understanding of the competition, whether you are a football manager, marketing manager, entertainer, managing director, or prime minister. Some of the questions to ask might include:
  - Which competitors do customers consider in our category of brands?
  - What positioning strategies are the competitors using, and why?
  - What key messages are they sending to consumers?
  - What appears to be their competitive advantage and the key points of difference?
  - Why do customers buy from them?
  - What image do they currently have?

○ What differences do customers see between their brand and ours?
○ What competitor brand would they switch to if they moved from us?

One of the major problems that can arise here is deciding just who the competition is. This issue is particularly relevant for commercial brands, where the definition of categories becomes extremely important, but it does need to be considered in any positioning situation for public sector brands too. Taking a private sector example, if we were to ask people whether or not Elton John is in the category of "rock music entertainers," we would almost certainly answer "yes;" however, if we were to ask whether he is competing with The Rolling Stones, we would probably say "no." Definition of the product category is therefore a critical first stage in competitor analysis, and is vital to the positioning effort. Even if the category is the same, it is still worthwhile to ask if the "competitor" really is a threat or an opportunity.

- *Why your brand is different from and better than the competition:* Analysis of the above areas will allow you to make some accurate judgements as to what position to choose and which positioning strategy you need to employ in order to influence the perceptions of the target audience(s).
- *The desired perception you would like people to have of your brand:* Always set a goal in terms of how you want to be seen by people. When you are writing down this goal, try to do it using the language of the customer or the people you are trying to influence. If you put yourself in their shoes, there is a greater likelihood that you will understand how they think and be successful in managing their perceptions, and you will find it easier to track whether you have achieved the intended image. When you write your positioning statement, certain things contained in it may be aspirational in nature and some factual. This doesn't matter, as these statements are for internal purposes only. However, the aspirational or desired consumer perceptions must be worked on hard in order to deliver on the promise. Communicating parts

of the positioning may have to be delayed, therefore, until the brand can actually do what it says it can, and if there are any aspirational elements to the positioning statement, these should be noted at the end of the document. This is especially important as positioning statements form an important part of any communications or creative brief given to external agencies and the notes will guide them not only in what words and phrases mean but also in what is aspirational at present and so cannot be used in creative execution.

Some of the above analysis might entail commissioned research if you don't have the internal resources to carry it out and it may take some time, but the quality of your communicated position will end up much more focused and accurate. Once you are ready to write the positioning statement, it has to be done in a concise way.

How to write a positioning statement

There are many ways of writing positioning statements but they should all draw on the elements mentioned above. From past experience, I have found the following template to be the most practical.

Note on the brand personality (character)

This is the personality your brand has, as discussed in the previous chapter. This can be stated separately at the end of the positioning statement; or more usefully, the words that describe the personality can be used in the text of the positioning statement itself.

If you methodically work through this statement, you will achieve answers to the two main questions mentioned earlier, namely:

- Why is our brand better?
- Why is our brand different?

A POSITIONING STATEMENT TEMPLATE

BRAND X
is better than

COMPETITIVE SET
(The main competitors your brand is competing against in your category, industry etc.)
for

TARGET MARKET
(The customer group or groups you are aiming for stated, if possible, in terms of their needs and wants. For a master brand this would be broad, but for each customer segment it would be more clearly defined.)
because it

STRATEGIC COMPETITIVE ADVANTAGE (SCA)
(The SPECIFIC advantage(s) your brand has, compared to others, in meeting those needs.)
with the result that

KEY PROPOSITION
(emphasizing the real emotional, and wherever possible, rational benefits to be experienced by your target audience, derived mainly from the SCA.)

You will also be very clear about the benefits consumers will enjoy from being a customer of your brand. At the end of the day all customers or prospective customers want to know what is in it for them. Consumers want to know why they should buy your brand in preference to others on offer. Only if these questions are answered truthfully and adequately will you be able to persuade customers that you should be their preferred choice. Great care must therefore be taken to ensure that the content of positioning statements is credible, believable, deliverable, and relevant to the wants and needs of the audience whose perceptions you are trying to influence.

CASE STUDY: An Airline's Positioning Statement

In this particular public sector example, you will see the master brand positioning statement for an Asian airline, a government-linked organization, aimed at expressing how it is different and better than other international carriers. You will also see how this can then be transferred down into positioning statements for each target audience. It is important in positioning statements to go into detail for segments because their needs and wants are different and so your total proposition will be geared to suit them. However, the segment positioning statements take direction from the master brand statement to ensure consistency while also ensuring relevance.

This is a real case that addresses all major segments of the market. The main things consumers look for when choosing to travel with airlines are safety, convenience, and a great brand experience via service, whether pre-flight, in-flight, or post-flight. You will find this reflected in the statements. You will also notice that the brand's strategic competitive advantage is carried throughout the different statements.

It should be noted that the airline brand and its competitors were defined in the actual positioning statements but have been withheld from this version due to confidentiality agreements.[8]

---

[8] This case study is reproduced from Temporal, Paul, *Advanced Brand Management: Managing Brands in a Changing World*, John Wiley & Sons (Asia) Pte Ltd, 2010.

MASTER BRAND POSITIONING STATEMENT

AIRLINE BRAND X

is better than

OTHER INTERNATIONAL CARRIERS

for

ALL USERS OF AIRLINE SERVICES

because it

Employs state-of-the-art systems and technology, with global
presence, complemented by the naturalness, warmth, and traditions
of service of a national personality that represents the very best of *all*
of Asia

with the result that

Every customer can have complete confidence in the understanding
of their personal needs and wants and the natural, genuine
willingness of Airline X people to care.

Note: This is a very general statement to cover all segments but the key strategic competitive advantages are present. These are then applied to the different customer segments.

When the brand has been positioned in this way these statements must then be applied rigorously to product, service, staff, communications, etc. In other words, the brand must be brought to life and the promises delivered upon. This brand strategy was built to enhance the image of a national airline that possessed some strengths but also some negative perceptions that could be improved upon.

Companies, institutions, organizations and countries often find themselves with an image that needs to be changed through repositioning as mentioned earlier. This is often as a result of perceptions from past experiences, policies and other factors.

ECONOMY CLASS POSITIONING STATEMENT

AIRLINE BRAND X

is better than

Every other international carrier

for

Those seeking a comfortable, safe, convenient journey that offers new standards in air travel with a fascinating cultural dimension

because it

Employs state-of-the-art systems and technology, complemented by the naturalness, warmth, and traditions of service of a national personality that represents the very best of *all* of Asia

with the result that

Their voyage becomes a unique experience and a lasting memory.

BUSINESS CLASS POSITIONING STATEMENT

AIRLINE BRAND X

is better than

Every other international carrier

for

Business Class travellers seeking a vastly enhanced experience of pure enjoyment

because it

Offers all the Business Class space, luxury, and special features expected of a sophisticated global airline, made truly special by the naturalness, warmth, and service traditions of a national personality that represents the very best of *all* of Asia

with the result that

They arrive happier, more refreshed, and more relaxed, having enjoyed a superior form of delivery of all the privileges and attention they deserve.

FIRST CLASS POSITIONING STATEMENT

AIRLINE BRAND X
is better than

Every other international carrier
for

Those seeking absolute luxury, convenience, privacy, and individual recognition
because it

Offers unique First Class privileges and, in the naturalness, warmth, and service of their attendants, an incomparable experience of Asia
with the result that

Their flight becomes "a journey" in indulgence – given colour and excitement by the fascinating traditions and combined personalities of the world's most exotic continent.

Below are two case studies for the public sector brand of Britain. Both show how branding has been used to reposition Britain by focusing on deliverable brand values that are inherent but not perceived as such by different countries in Asia, and where the perceptions were predominant.

One is concerned with how Britain is viewed in Asia and how a brand building exercise was carried out to strengthen and change perceptions, and the second one is an example of how to take one brand personality characteristic that is very important to the country but poorly perceived, and totally change that perception starting with one Asian country and then rolling the strategy out globally.

CASE STUDIES: Repositioning Britain in Asia

Case Study 1: Britain in Asia

In one Asian country this was taken up by the British Government as a specific brand project – to address the brand strengths and weaknesses of Britain, and formulate a comprehensive plan to change market perceptions, using Malaysia as the first country.

The vision and values

The first step toward achieving this was to establish a vision for the brand, based around the concept of "a close and trusted friend." Then came the creation of a set of core brand values in the form of a strong but demonstrable personality that would serve as the basis for many campaigns to come in the next few years. These brand values were defined carefully to ensure total commitment from all stakeholders.

Four core values were chosen to portray Britain, British companies, British products and services, and the British as a nation of people. These would enhance the strengths of the brand image already perceived and change some of the less desirable elements. These were:

- innovative
- dependable
- professional
- stylish

Careful deliberation and much debate went into this choice. The values had to be believable, credible and capable of being demonstrated by all stakeholders in one form or another both now and in the years ahead.

Inclusivity was important for the brand to have buy-in and be applied consistently and also to serve as a brand management tool.

Thus the British High Commission, the British Tourist Authority, the British Council, the country's British Industry and Trade Association, the North West Arts Board, British communications specialists living in the country, British Airways and other key industry leaders were all involved in the process.

Positioning and key messages

Various target audiences were defined, and a master brand positioning statement was written that was applicable to all, with minor modifications for each segment. The format used was the template described above.

The key positioning advantage that Britain felt it had was "friendship." This was based on historical circumstances (Commonwealth ties), strong government relations and trade, and a genuine affection for the people of each country by the other. It was decided to develop a series of key messages for each separate target audience by defining the brand personality characteristics and bringing in the friendship dimension. Some examples of the key messages that were to be projected were:

- *Innovative:* state-of-the-art technology, creativity in ideas, flexibility in structures and business activities.
- *Dependability:* long-term historical relationship between Britain and Malaysia, long-term commitment, familiarity with systems and language.
- *Professional:* trustworthiness and reliability, performing to high standards, quality of training and education.
- *Stylish:* trendsetting, fun, excellence, elegance, heritage.

From these examples you will see that there is a combination of the old and the new – tradition and modernity, showing the best of the past and the present British nation.

(continued)

Visual identity

Finally, a logo was designed to encapsulate all the values and the positioning, and a tagline to summarize the brand was created namely, "Just Between Friends."

Brand and campaign management

Since the brand was established in 1998, there have been several campaigns and activities. During the first year, special attention was given to ensuring that everyone was briefed on the brand and the reasons for its creation and values. This not only applied to British institutions and companies already in Malaysia, but to organizers and sponsors of every subsequent trade, promotion, arts or other events. Briefing kits were produced and all were encouraged to incorporate the brand and its elements into their advertising and promotional activities. The logo was mandatory. In this way, every visitor from trade mission members to Whitehall officials married their messages to the overall Britain-in-Malaysia messaging.

As the then British High Commissioner to Malaysia, Sir David Moss, said in a major public speech prior to the first of the brand campaigns, "We have, over the past months, been developing a strategy to promote the campaign. We have sought out expert advice and have come up with a set of values which we believe suitably stress why Britain is better and unique... These ambitious goals equate to a major programme of arts, educational, and trade-related events. If presented professionally and backed by a consistent message from all those in the British community, they will significantly raise the profile and image of Britain... As any company will testify, the application of a key set of values in a consistent year-on-year fashion has proved to be the best investment in image-building that they can make. By consistently stressing why Britain is different and better through the values we have identified, we shall provide the strategic platform for the successful presentation of all British activity in Malaysia."

The brand has remained relevant as he said it would. Importantly, it brought tremendous results in all areas of British activity, and still continues to be a driving force in the development of an even stronger image for Britain.

CASE STUDY: Innovation UK in Japan

A similar brand strategy initiative was begun in 2003 and has continued since that date to reposition Britain as an innovative nation. The initiative was launched in a country which is inclined, because of its own prowess in this competency, to believe that this is far from the truth – Japan. Even though Britain has probably been one of the most innovative countries in the world's history, Japanese perceptions run deep and this is a great branding challenge. Following the launch of the brand in Japan, Innovation UK was rolled out across many countries of the world with whom Britain wants to do business.

Japan and the UK have some similarities. Both are a collection of islands, both combine monarchy with democracy, and both have imperial pasts and strong traditions of craft-based businesses. That is more or less where the commonality ends as culturally they are very different, and the common heritage between the two does not in any way mean that UK businesses have an "inside track" to winning business in Japan. To the Japanese, being "British" is not necessarily an attractive differentiator for UK companies, as the UK is not perceived as being really innovative.

The Japanese have very clear ideas of what they want and very often whom they are prepared to buy it from. They like to buy original and unique things, and have a keen interest in innovation and winning in global markets; they will buy what they need from wherever they can find the best. This has led the British Government to try and change the perceptions of the Japanese towards the UK as far as

(continued)

innovation goes, in an attempt to boost trade in design and related fields in the world's second largest economy. The project was called "Innovation UK," and the brand strategy and concept have become a huge operation across the world.

Using similar methodology to that described above in the first case study, a set of brand values was elicited and a positioning statement written for all sectors and organizations to follow. These also determined the design elements for the Innovation UK campaign.

Brand personality

A set of brand values in the form of personality characteristics was created that were deliverable and which were used to bring out the tone, manner, look and feel of all the Innovation UK communications. The emotional ones were made to take preference as they were likely to have most impact and also act as a brand differentiator.

- *Rational:* creative, resourceful, intelligent.
- *Emotional:* visionary, passionate, inspiring, happy and open about sharing ideas.

Different communications emphasize different parts of the personality, but the friendly tone and manner should always shine through, as this is a major part of the UK personality in Asia. Thus the brand personality can be thought of as a "brand chord" where some keys can be played louder than others depending on the nature of the target audience and the subject matter of the communications. However, over time all of the personality traits must be portrayed.

Brand positioning

A master brand positioning statement was drawn up to cover all target audiences and guide all messaging and events. It was necessarily broad, but capable of modification to suit individual audiences.

Innovation UK Brand Positioning Statement

UK
is better than

ALL OTHER COUNTRIES
for

Governments, investors, businesses, R&D institutions and technology professionals, students, and any organizations in Japan looking for inspiration, technology breakthroughs and visionary ideas that will shape the world in which we live
because

Not only do we have proven authenticity as a source of scientific and technology ideas, products and innovative practice, we also have a passion to share our ideas and breakthroughs with others in order to enrich the quality of life for all citizens of the world
with the result that

We offer hope, optimism, opportunities and excitement to those who want to make a real difference to people's lives and tomorrow's world.

At first sight, this positioning may well look to be difficult to deliver and brand communications had to clearly spell out why the UK was able to hold this position. The fact that the UK was not seen as at all innovative was entirely a perception issue. Facts such as the following were portrayed at all events accompanied by creative execution. At that time, the UK:

- Was approaching 100 Nobel prize winners in the field of science.
- Had a tradition of leadership in science and technology including Newton's gravitation and laws of motion, Darwin's work, Faraday's electricity applications, Fleming's discovery of penicillin, Watson and Crick's discovery of DNA, Hodgkin's discovery of cholesterol and insulin, and the cloning of animals.

- The inventions of radio, computers and fibre-optic cables, and Baird's first demonstration of television in 1926.
- Prominence of British people in running fashion houses.
- The domination of music and musical innovation by British artists.

The final list was longer than this, but the UK's position as a source of innovation and creativity could not be challenged on this basis. The fact that this was not recognized in Japan or globally was a matter of perception, and somewhat modest communications.

The launch event involved a video message by Prime Minister Tony Blair at a reception for over 400 top government and industry people. At all subsequent Innovation UK brand events, the positioning has been reinforced by customer satisfaction surveys carried out and the ratings have always been extremely high. Furthermore, Innovation UK has been a major commercial success for Britain with many joint ventures, increased trade and investment and other relationships. As a spokesperson for UK Trade and Investment said, "Innovation drives economic progress. For businesses it will mean sustained or improved growth. For consumers, it will mean higher-quality and better-value goods, more efficient services and higher standards of living. To the economy as a whole, innovation is the key to higher productivity." Referring to the development and implementation of the brand strategy, Brian Ferrar from the UK Foreign and Commonwealth Office said, "Defining our brand strategy was an essential prerequisite in promoting the UK as an innovative country. Setting out a clear proposition helped us to ensure that our activities were targeted at the right audiences in the right way. Paul Temporal helped greatly in this process which has resulted in tremendous gains in terms of stronger business relationships and international collaborations."

The conclusion from these examples is that countries undoubtedly realize the power of branding techniques and will increasingly use these to manage the perceptions of audiences they wish to reach. Inclusivity is important; all affected and interested parties must be involved in the brand creation process if it is to maintain momentum and commitment. As time advances, nations will find their images are those of the past, and they will need to reposition themselves to address the needs of markets that change very fast and competition that becomes increasingly aggressive. Britain is doing just that in several areas of the world.

Repositioning – the new paradigm

Ten to twenty years ago repositioning was an event that was fairly unusual, driven mainly by the reasons described above, but in the present day it is becoming more frequent as companies seek to keep up with the pace of change and innovation. As constant innovation becomes mandatory for success, so repositioning follows in an equally mandatory manner. Repositioning of brands is now the norm rather than the exception, taking place on a much more frequent basis, and this means that brand managers have to take a different view of how they sustain and improve their market leadership and/or ambitions.

Factors to consider in repositioning your brand in the world of change are:

- Accept that repositioning is an essential part of brand development.
- Ensure you don't alter the personality of your product/service/ organization, as this will place your brand in the "unpredictable" category.
- Gather market intelligence on what the changing needs of your customers are, and the competitive response.
- Remember you are dealing in the management of perceptions, and this means that you must budget for it – repositioning means cash outflow in image and product communications to change perceptions and make people *think* you are still, or are now, different and better. The more entrenched the perceptions are, the more you will have to spend.

- Bear in mind that all the products/services you have in the pipeline might need to be changed or adjusted according to your new positioning; if this is difficult, then your repositioning may encounter problems. In the case of major items such as infrastructure, for instance, this can take several years, whereas the introduction of new technology may be able to be changed more quickly.
- Get buy-in from everyone that can make an impact on the brand in your company, or the repositioning effort will not work.
- Remember the basics: in order to reposition, you either have to add more value to the brand proposition for existing target audiences, or look at capturing another target audience.

Should positioning be revolutionary or evolutionary?

"Revolutionary positioning" is a term that tends to be applied to a situation where you are starting from square one, say with a new product, company, or personal goal. In such a situation there is no current image, and a position has to be created for the first time. In other words, once you are nowhere, you have to go somewhere. In this case positioning has to be revolutionary. You have to choose a powerful position amid all the established competitors, and make an impact.

"Evolutionary positioning," on the other hand, is about developing your image gradually. Here the issue is that once you are somewhere, you have to decide where to go next and not be left behind. This is a repositioning problem and it can be extremely dangerous. The danger lies in suddenly stepping completely away from the position you have been occupying, and to which consumers, particularly existing customers, are accustomed to, without alienating them and losing your unique identity.

In most cases, brand managers have the dilemma of balancing the two approaches. For example, Georgio Armani, in an interview with CNN, described his biggest problem as how to keep his classic design styling while at the same time adopting fashionable change. He saw it as a true dichotomy. On the one hand, the existing customer base expects to see his classic style. On the other hand, fashion is moving faster, due to technological advances and media hype. Armani said that the media are now less sensitive to individual style and more attuned to what mass designers are producing. So if the mass-design latest fashions include the colour red, everyone (Armani included) is expected to deliver something in red. If not, he said, he would be left out of media support for that season. The dilemma for designers like Armani, therefore, is how to remain true to his distinctive style – that is *positioning* – and yet incorporate the latest trends. His answer is: evolutionary change not revolutionary change. He has to position his products to satisfy the conflict of identity versus modernity. He must remain constant to his customers and meet their expectations both of classic style and contemporary fashion.

Positioning for equality

Time passes quickly, and people's wants, needs, and aspirations change over time. Sometimes you just have to accept the fact that you are falling (or already are) behind the pack, and have to catch up. You have to convince people that you are "with it," not out of touch with the latest trend, are up-to-date, contemporary, and can match what others offer. This means positioning for equality – showing people that you aren't disadvantaged.

Quite often this type of positioning is concerned with the more basic competitive elements of features and benefits, and keeping up with the needs and wants of the people you are trying to retain or acquire as customers. It is also mostly confined to positioning against the competition in specific categories, such as personal computers. With this category the life cycles have shortened so much that when customers start to use their left brain and analyze and justify which particular brand's features and benefits will both do the job and give value for money, the next range of upgraded models have already made the choice obsolete.

Positioning here then, is aimed at giving your customers the message that you have the necessary elements to be a legitimate competitor in that specific area of interest. So, as a computer manufacturer or retailer, you have to have models with the latest chips, hard disk sizes, memory capabilities, speed, and so on. Public sector organizations must also keep up with change, especially regarding the needs and wants of current and potential customers.

Positioning for superiority

Everyone likes to be superior, the best, everyone's choice, but this position is difficult to create and maintain. It goes far beyond equality positioning by seeking to create inequality, a differential advantage, and an image of being a cut above the rest, an undisputed leader. Some organizations, including several of the world's leading brands, have already done this. Others have it firmly placed on their boardroom agenda.

Positioning for superiority is only achievable once the target audience acknowledges equality. In other words, you have to demonstrate that you are at least as good as the competition with whatever it is you are offering, and only then can you persuade people that you really have something extra or special to give.

Public sector institutions that gain a superior position can be said to have achieved a sustainable competitive advantage (SCA), being the most preferred choice in their field of competition.

Evaluate brand positioning regularly

I would like to re-emphasize that positioning is the one part of the brand strategy that can change, and change frequently, as explained in the section called Repositioning earlier in this chapter. The other two essentials of a brand strategy – the brand vision and values or personality – tend not to. The point to be made here is that whatever your brand positioning is, it needs to be evaluated against the competition and the changing needs of consumers on a regular basis, at least annually.

Summary

- In developing any public sector brand strategy the process necessary to achieve success is the same as that used in the private sector. We saw in Chapter 4 that the first two steps in brand strategy creation involve brand visions, values and personalities. The third step is to create a powerful position.
- Brand positioning brings into play the competition and here it is important to establish what the strategic competitive advantage of the brand is compared to those competitors.
- The best way to do this is to create a positioning statement that describes why your brand is different and better than that of competitors. You may need more than one positioning statement for different target audiences but the central key message referring to that advantage should remain the same.
- In developing the positioning of the brand always ensure that there is inclusivity of all stakeholders so that anyone who can influence the brand, and make an impact on it, are committed to what is written and are prepared to deliver on it.
- Once the brand strategy is clearly defined and agreed by all, you will find that this acts as a clear guide for implementation using internal and external resources.
- At least once a year, ensure that your brand positioning is still relevant, as market dynamics, customer needs, and competitive activity can change with reasonable frequency. At some stage you may need to reposition your brand depending on whether your present position is less strong, less relevant, or under attack from competitors.

Part Two of this book contains four chapters that focus on implementation of the strategy and the management of the brand. Chapter 6 provides a holistic view of how a brand should be managed. Chapter 7 looks at brand communications, and Chapter 8 deals with internal brand engagement. Chapter 9 takes a brief look at how brand success can be measured.

Part Two

Implementing and Managing Public Sector Brands

P art One of the book dealt with the background of why brands are important to the public sector and how strong brands are built by looking at visions, personality, values, and positioning techniques; in other words, strategy. This section is concerned with the implementation and management of brand strategy. All implementation of brand strategy falls under the heading of brand management, but there are different aspects involved in the management of brands as can be seen in the following diagram.

As most experienced brand managers know, the implementation and management of strategy is no easy task as there are many variables that can influence the final brand image and whether it matches the desired brand identity. Some of these variables may be under the control of brand managers but some may not, and this is what makes the role of a brand manager so very difficult.

This section will explore the many variables that impact on brands to be developed and managed in the public sector, and will consist of four chapters. The first chapter (Chapter 6) will focus on the broad issues involved in managing brands including brand management structure, while the second and third (Chapters 7 and 8) will home in on brand communications and brand engagement.

After these, the section will end with Chapter 9 that deals with how to measure brand success, and looks in detail at brand valuation methodology. One of the recent steps forward in branding in both public and private sectors is the development of globally-recognized techniques to value brands financially using the data to examine the drivers of brand value, and so improve value creation. I will include nation branding as a public sector example together with a look at the 2013 top 100 Nation Brand index produced by Brand Finance plc (BrandFinance® *Nation Brands 100*).

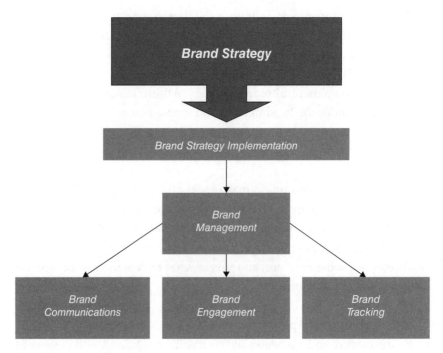

Brand Strategy and Implementation

Chapter 6

Public Sector Brand Management

So far, the book has referred to the need for, and the development of, brand strategy. This chapter deals with the issue of brand management. The need for focused communications and internal engagement will be outlined in detail later but all implementation initiatives come under the broad heading of brand management. I will now look at the range of activities that brand managers have to deal with and the necessity to have a solid structure to deal with the management of brands.

What is brand management?

Put very simply, brand management is a process that tries to take control over everything a brand does and says, and the way in which it is perceived. There is a need therefore, to influence the perceptions of various target audiences to ensure that people see what you want them to see with respect to your brand. This means, as we have seen earlier in the book, identifying clearly what your brand stands for, its personality, and how to position it so that it appears different and better than competing brands. It involves integrated communications, and constant engagement of customers, partners and employees. But, as we shall see shortly, there are many other variables that need to be given attention.

The overall aim of the brand management process is to increase the value of the brand over time, however that may be measured. Profitability can be one measure, market share another, volume of sales or number of visitors another and the emotional associations of the brand with consumers (often referred to as brand equity) yet another. But one of the hardest parts of brand management is to achieve a balance between the short-term quantitative goals often demanded by top management to satisfy various stakeholders, and the long-term growth of the brand and its value.

For example, price-cutting might buy short-term market share but at what cost to the brand's long-term image? For government-related companies that are often listed there is the need to perform to stock market requirements on a quarterly basis in terms of sales and profitability whilst maintaining or even increasing investment in the brands that deliver results. There can therefore, be conflicts of interest between the needs of the business and growth of the brands.

In the public sector other challenges can also arise. These include the existence of intra-brand competition, a lack of inclusiveness of all stakeholders, balancing long-term policies with short-term objectives, and many other issues including brand guardianship.

As you will now have begun to see, brand management is a difficult job. What makes it more difficult is the fact that many of the elements that influence a brand's success are often outside the control of those responsible for its management, such as competitor moves, economic factors, and consumer trends. Proactivity and reactivity live side by side in the daily work of brand managers, and this is the very reason that makes brand management so exciting – brands live in ever-changing landscapes, full of opportunities and challenges.

I will explain some of these issues by using a model I have developed called the Brand Management Wheel.

The Brand Management Wheel

The Brand Management Wheel is a model that is used by brand managers in both public and private sectors to understand all the elements that can make an impact on the image of their brand. Those responsible for a brand can add in particular elements relevant to them when considering how to try and manage the image of their brand, but here are some examples.

Figure 6.1 features some of the main elements that can affect a national brand strategy and its consequent image. Some of these are "givens" and reflect the culture and broad personality of the country and its people, while others are more adaptable to change. Some can be changed in the relative short term while others require a longer time.

For example, it is difficult to change the natural friendliness of people in a nation and how welcoming they are, but with public diplomacy initiatives and policies that make things easy for businesses and visitors,

Figure 6.1 The Brand Management Wheel.

a country can appear quite welcoming. One could say that the British are not perhaps renowned for out-and-out friendliness as a cultural trait, but the massive amount of policy and training initiatives demonstrated in the 10 years up to and including the 2012 Olympic Games eventually showed how welcoming Britain could be.

Examples of other changes taking a long time are the provision of infrastructure and political stability, although the latter can sometimes not be too critical in achieving national objectives as Thailand currently proves. An example of change that can be accomplished in a shorter time frame is the use of brand ambassadors and brand differentiation strategies and communications.

The essential driving force behind most of these items is the existence of economic policies and diplomacy. If government is not willing to ensure that pro-business, pro-visitor and pro-talent policies are put in place then it is difficult to execute a friendly brand strategy.

Managing brand touchpoints

'A more focused example is shown in Figure 6.2 where, by looking at all the touchpoints a ministry or government department has in the pursuit' of foreign trade, the wheel can act as the architect of a well-orchestrated brand implementation strategy.

Brand touchpoints exist whenever anyone comes into contact or interacts with a brand in any of its manifestations. Brand owners and managers often conduct a rigorous analysis of customer touchpoints in order to manage the brand consistently and communicate the right messages.

In addition, looking at various brand touchpoints such as these can be a useful way of monitoring brand performance and assessing the competition. In the private sector, global brands, such as Philips, use touchpoint analysis for exactly these purposes; they assess by meticulous research how well they

Figure 6.2 Influencing Brand Touchpoints.

perform against their competitors on each touchpoint along the customer journey, from pre-purchase to purchase and post-purchase activities.

As with all brand management opportunities and activities the aim is to generate consistent and differentiated brand development and a better customer experience. Even with a focused example like the trade and industry one above, it is clear that a great deal of work has to be carried out that will need to include a great many people in the brand development process. This means that there must be a structure in place in order to ensure that everything is "on strategy," that existing challenges are dealt with, new and innovative ideas are implemented, and that success is monitored. This is often referred to as brand guardianship.

Brand guardianship and structure

Brand guardianship is a vital function and without it a brand strategy left unmanaged may well go astray with the brand image developing in an ad hoc and unfocused way. Large companies in the private sector usually ensure that brand guardianship is well-organized, but in the public sector that is not always the case. In order to be clear, it is important that some kind of brand management or guardianship structure is established as soon as possible in the stages of brand development.

Before looking at structure, there are challenges that strong brand management can bring to the table in terms of brand building. One is ensuring inclusiveness and the other is minimizing or eradicating intra-brand competition.

Inclusiveness

When formulating or implementing a brand strategy it is critical to include all stakeholders who can make a positive or negative impact on the brand. This has been referred to in earlier chapters and a good brand management structure will ensure this happens. For example, in the development and implementation of the national brand of South Africa (Brand South Africa) this custodial function was allocated to the International Marketing Council of South Africa (IMC). This case also illustrates how the brand can be developed in an evolutionary way and not a revolutionary way.

CASE STUDY: Brand South Africa

Brand South Africa says, "Brand South Africa was established in August 2002 to help create a positive and compelling brand image for South Africa.

"At that time, the world was unsure about what to think of South Africa, with many different messages being sent out by various sources. This did very little to build the country's brand and it was evident that to attract tourism and investment there was a need to coordinate marketing initiatives to make them more effective.

"This led to the creation of Brand South Africa, whose main objective is the marketing of South Africa through the Brand South Africa campaign.

"There are many benefits to having a consolidated brand image, with the most important being that a consistent Brand South Africa message creates strategic advantages in terms of trade and tourism for the country in an increasingly competitive marketplace."[1]

The International Marketing Council (IMC) was responsible for Brand South Africa's development and its roles when starting the branding process were:

1. **To help develop a master (they called it "mother") brand proposition for South Africa.** In carrying out this task there was an intensive effort to research and consult with as many local and international stakeholders as possible across social, political, economic, business, media, citizens, tourists and other influencers. Several positioning statements were tested in this process, and the outcome was the stated Brand South Africa brand essence of "South Africa, Alive with Possibility."

2. **To work on the brand architecture and define the relationship between the master brand and its sub-brands such as tourism and business.** The inclusiveness of the first step ensured that good commitment and buy-in was given by sub-brands in understanding the master brand and how they could use various elements of it to mutual advantage. In other words, it was clear how the sub-brands could exercise autonomy while still adhering to the proposition of the master brand.

3. **To help define the strategy to be followed in achieving certain objectives.** This was mainly brand communications strategy aimed at both local and international markets, but also included initiatives such as the involvement of brand ambassadors and overseas missions.

(continued)

---

[1] www.brandsouthafrica.com/who-we-are

4. **To track progress.** In terms of guardianship, IMC was to be the custodian of the master brand and sub-brands would be represented by their stakeholders. IMC conducted a national perception audit, which measured important brand attributes and how well they were being delivered on, and an international brand equity study, which measured Brand South Africa's health against that of competitors.

Brand development

The work done from 2002–2006 was regarded as a good basis for establishing the brand prior to the major event of the FIFA Soccer World Cup in 2010. In March 2010 a new CEO of IMC was appointed, but the purpose of Brand South Africa remained the same.

"Brand South Africa works closely with a number of partners in building a positive, unified image of South Africa; one that builds pride, promotes investment and tourism, and helps new enterprises and job creation. We are proud to support, and be supported by, the Office of the Presidency, the South African Government, the Department of Trade and Industry (DTI), Government Communication and Information System (GCIS) and South African Tourism."[2]

However, the proposition that IMC developed, changed from the original slogan, "Alive with Possibilities" to a new slogan launched by Brand South Africa in 2012 called, "South Africa – Inspiring New Ways."

In 2012, "Inspiring New Ways" became the new marketing slogan for South African Tourism, which was developed as a result of extensive research and consultation. The aim was to find a flexible expression of the brand positioning for South Africa that depicts how South Africans continually generate new ways of overcoming challenges and finding solutions in an ever-changing world. It had to represent more than just tourism.

---

[2] www.brandsouthafrica.com/who-we-are/stakeholders

In a press release, Brand South Africa CEO, Miller Matola, explained how South Africa had evolved in stature and confidence, and so there was a need to review the brand in order to reflect how the country has developed. Matola described how the repositioning of the brand would need to "support marketing South Africa as an investment destination, and to promote our products and services. It also had to mobilize support from South Africans at home and abroad."[3] Improvements in South Africa's rankings in finance and governance in the World Economic Forum's 2011/12 Global Competitiveness report supported this wider positioning for the brand.

Matola acknowledged that other countries on the continent have also become very competitive which meant there was a need to differentiate themselves as a "more grown-up" nation, "where we are not still talking of 'possibilities' 18 years into democracy and re-entering the international community." He further explained that the progression from "possibility to delivery" had implications for Brand South Africa as it had changed, just as the country had; and he credited South Africa for its highly regarded tourism industry, excellent banking and financial regulation which pointed to a country that delivered as opposed to having "possibilities".

Intra-brand competition and inclusiveness

The notion of inclusiveness, developing a brand for all stakeholders in the country based on consultation and research ably demonstrated in the Brand South Africa case, ensures that not only do all sub-brands keep in step with master brands but that brands do not compete directly against each other in their communications. While sub-brands often compete for government revenue and talent, this can sometimes be wasteful.

---

[3] www.brandsouthafrica.com/news/792-inspiration-behind-the-brand

For example, in Singapore all three armed forces have, on several occasions, advertised on national television and in other media for talent, an exercise which was not just costly, but neutralizing in their effect, becoming a competition of creative execution. In tourism there is also a tendency for different destinations within a nation to compete and carry out substantial brand campaigns that do little to contribute to the key message and positioning of the master brand. Australia and Malaysia have both experienced this in the past with different territories and states respectively carrying different messages, logos, visual identity and brand propositions, and communicating these to the same target audiences in order to reach their own market objectives in terms of visitors.

The only way in which synergistic brand behaviour can be minimized is through the establishment of a good brand guardianship structure with all stakeholders represented.

Brand management structure

In the private sector, product groups or ranges often have their own Product Brand Committees to ensure that everything the brand does is in line with its strategy. An example of this would be the Nescafé product brand range. For corporate brands there is often a two-tier structure. As brands are top-down driven but need to engage all stakeholders, it is sensible to have this relationship reflected in the management of the brand. In organizations I have worked with in the public and private sectors, we have implemented this by having a Brand Management Council or Brand Management Committee (BMC) at the most senior level and a Brand Working Committee (BWC) that covers the rest of the hierarchy and functions across the organization. There can be a variety of roles played by either of these bodies but below are some examples of ones that do exist.

BMC roles

The Brand Management Council/Committee (BMC) is very strategic and can often be an extension of a management committee or executive committee that makes decisions on the business and operational aspects of the organization. Its roles in the management of the brand are usually:

1. To determine the architecture of the brands under their control and to ensure that brand discipline and consistency is adhered to across the organization. Brand discipline will include the prevention of new logos and brands that do not fit with the master brand from being introduced. It will also ensure that new brands, which are approved, adhere to the rules of the brand architecture.

2. To establish and confirm all aspects of brand strategy and set the strategic direction for brand communication initiatives. This includes both internal communications involving staff, and external communications involving the various stakeholders.

3. Exercise the final veto on major initiatives affecting brand image, for example, major advertising campaigns. The BMC must have the authority to stop any major initiatives that may have a detrimental effect on the overall brand image. This will ascertain that a consistent brand image is being communicated to various stakeholders and markets.

4. To review and monitor all internal and external brand communications performance. This will include internal brand communications (e.g. newsletter, intranet, email, poster campaigns, competitions, and so on), as well as external communications (e.g. corporate visual identity, public relations, sponsorships, event management, corporate website, use of Internet websites and so on).

5. To provide advice to the various subcommittees on branding issues. That is, it will ensure all decisions put forward by the various subcommittees are in line with the brand strategy of the organization.

6. To approve co-branding, strategic alliances, and major partnership initiatives. This will ensure that partner brands selected to work with

the organization will not transfer any negative elements to the brand. Concurrently, the organization should benefit from leveraging on some of the positive associations linked to its branded partners.

7. To be responsible for selecting and briefing future brand partners on relevant aspects of the brand. This will ascertain that future brand partners comprehend the values and identity of the brand, and help prevent them from misrepresenting the brand in any negative way.

8. To evaluate and approve all brand plans put forward by the BWC. With this, the BMC will prioritize and filter various brand-related initiatives put forward. This will help to optimize use of resources and utilization of budgets, and maximize impact on corporate image.

9. To allocate financial resources for brand development. That is, the BMC will evaluate initiatives and budgets put forward by the BWC. For initiatives that are approved by the BMC, the BMC will put up the respective budget to the management committee or board for approval. Annual brand-related spending would normally be put up in one budget.

10. To be accountable and responsible for the organization's competitive identity and the positioning of the brand in all markets. This will include approving all business and market development activities that will have an impact on how the brand is being portrayed and positioned. For new markets to be developed, the BMC will have to consider new sub- positioning issues.

11. To ensure clear reporting and tracking mechanisms for all brand initiatives are in place. It has to ensure that it receives consistent updates on all initiatives that have an impact on the brand. In addition, it has to track how the perception of the brand is changing with the entry of new competitors and initiatives taken. With this, the BMC will be able to monitor the effectiveness of the various brand-related initiatives that have been introduced.

12. To be responsible for ensuring that all branding activities are related and linked to any performance management or scorecard systems.

The relationship between the BMC and the BWC is shown in Figure 6.3.

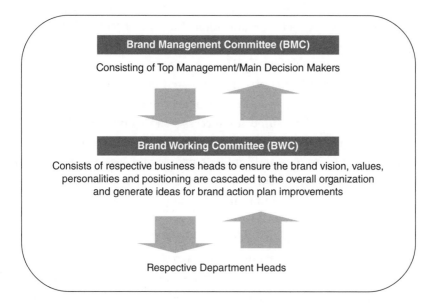

Figure 6.3 The relationship between brand management and working committees.

BWC roles

The main aim of a Brand Working Committee (BWC) is to provide operational information and comprehensive brand action plans for the brand to the BMC (Brand Management Council/Committee). A BWC provides information and responds to requests on subjects such as market research, customer relationship management, brand tracking, design and packaging, all brand communications and new product development.

A BWC is also responsible for ensuring that everyone in the organization is trained in what the brand stands for and how they can play their part, and this applies to everyone in the organization in all departments and at all functions and levels. It is the idea generation team that gathers lots of plans and ideas and feeds these to the BMC in prioritized fashion, with time-scales and measurement criteria to allow the BMC to make informed decisions on all major brand activities. As an example, in one particular public sector organization after a newly set up BWC held a half-day ideas session with all departmental heads, over 130 possibilities for improving the brand image of the organization were identified. These were then separated into short-, medium- and long-term timeframes and more detail obtained on what the outcomes from these ideas should be, how they would be measured for success, who would lead the process and how much financial and human resources would be required. It does not take much to involve and motivate people and sessions of a consultative and creative nature like this can be extremely rewarding, the end result also ensuring that commitment and buy-in is there.

Whereas the BMC might meet on a quarterly basis, the BWC tend to meet on a monthly basis as there is a lot of work to do. This kind of detailed work needs a team of people to be involved but it works well. The BMC has the final say on which plans go ahead and gives the sign off. The more important and impactful ideas may need policy changes and the BMC may need to take these to a higher approving authority, such as an executive- or board-level entity. When I have set up these arrangements and structures in the past I have found it best to tie the BMC into that policy decision-making body to facilitate progress. This can be achieved by having the BMC agenda backed on to that of the executive committee or board. This sometimes works well as the top-level people are often similar in position.

One final point to mention is that a senior representative from the BWC should be a member of the BMC or at least attend BMC meetings in order to ensure good communication and understanding of the items to be discussed. Quite often a few members of the BWC are invited to attend relevant parts of the BMC meetings for discussion and explanation.

This kind of structure is favoured by the private sector and many public sector organizations. But even though inclusivity and consultation is a must, it cannot be disputed that brands have to be driven from the top of an organization and with nations this means the government, as will be seen in the next two case studies featuring Switzerland and South Korea.

CASE STUDY: South Korea's Presidential Council on Nation Branding

In 2008, President Lee Myung-bak announced on the sixty-third anniversary of Korean Independence Day that, "If we wish to be an advanced nation, we must improve our reputation in a groundbreaking manner. I will soon establish a Presidential Council on Nation Branding under the direct control of the president." And so the Presidential Council on Nation Branding (PCNB) was founded on 22 January 2009, to upgrade what Korea saw as its relatively undervalued nation brand and improve its management effectiveness. Although the country had made significant steps forward in political, social and cultural development, Korea felt it still had some way to go to reach the status it desired globally. One of the triggers for this was a nation brand research study that ranked Korea thirty-ninth, behind countries like Mexico, India, China and Egypt on various brand strength factors such as cultural appeal, governance, demand for exports and others, even though Korea is the thirteenth most powerful economy in the world. PCNB refers to nation branding as the likeability, credibility, and even the dignity of a country and aims to raise the global status of Korea by working on these elements.

Former Korea University President, Euh Yoon-Dae, became the first chairman of PCNB, which included 47 members, (16 senior government officials including eight ministers, and 31 from the private sector), and five teams responsible for: international co-operation, corporate and information technology, culture and tourism, the global community, and overall co-ordination. He said, "We will start various projects to promote Korea's global image and make it a more respected country. The council will

(continued)

strengthen cooperation with the private sector and municipal governments to help Korean firms and nationals get better treatment overseas. It will play a central role in reorganizing Korea's branding activities and creating positive images abroad for the world's thirteenth largest economy."

The Presidential Council on Nation Branding serves as a control tower that integrates and controls government-promoted services and aims to utilize citizens' potential and encourage nationwide participation in its efforts.

With a nation brand vision of "A reliable and dignified Korea" and core values of "Sharing, Consideration, Respect, Communication and Unity," its four strategic objectives are to:

1. Expand contribution to international society (expand Korea's role as a member of international society in order to ensure its responsibility).
2. Disseminate the value of traditional culture (promote an image of Korea as an economically advanced nation and raise awareness of the nation's cultural values).
3. Strengthen global communication (reinforce mutual understanding between Korea and global society based on Korea's improving popularity and reputation since the success of the G20 Seoul Summit).
4. Pursue nationwide integration (include active citizen participation and encourage national self-esteem).

Since its formation, PCNB has achieved a great deal but its efforts will continue. As the current chairman Samuel Koo says, "The Presidential Council on Nation Branding will work continuously with the people of South Korea so that our nation can truly become one of the most important leading countries in the world. This is an investment for our future."[4]

---

[4] http://17koreabrand.pa.go.kr/

As if to underline this fact, a survey by the PCNB found that consumers in Japan, Germany and the United States marked down the value of identical products 30% or more when they were told they came from Korea. Similarly, they found that countries with a strong brand image were more likely to attract foreign direct investment. The notion of country-of-origin remains important, even for developed economies.[5]

The private sector has also joined in the Korean nation brand monitoring activity. In 2009, Samsung Economic Research Institute (SERI) and PCNB jointly began an annual study of the nation brands of 50 countries. The rationale for this is explained by Lee Dong-Hun a research fellow at SERI who says, "Although the conventional measures of national power, including military and economic strength, and population and territory size, remain important in international relations, there is an increasing consensus on the importance of soft power, in particular 'nation brand'."

The resultant index (called SERI-PCNB NBDO) presents two main sets of data: "Dual" which measures image and substance; and "Octagon" that measures eight categories of economy/corporations, science/technology, infrastructure, policies/institutions, heritage, modern culture, people and celebrities. The SERI-PCNB NBDO nation brand ranking also contrasts its findings with key competitive indexes such as those produced by IMD and WEF. In 2012, Korea ranked thirteenth in overall substance and seventeenth in overall image, both improvements over 2011 scores.[6]

I will discuss the measurement of nation brands again in Chapter 9 and look at how the brand value of a nation brand is calculated. However, this case study demonstrates the importance to governments of the soft power of brand image.

---

[5] *Nation Branding: Shaking off the Korea Discount*, Knowledge@Wharton, 12 January 2011.

[6] www.asia.udp.cl/Informes/2013/KoreaEconomicTrends-SERI.pdf

The next case will also demonstrate government commitment to building and managing a national brand, approached in a somewhat different way.

CASE STUDY: Presence Switzerland

Presence Switzerland monitors and supports the image of Switzerland abroad, and implements the strategy of the Federal Council on Switzerland's communication abroad. It was created by a decision taken by the Swiss Federal Parliament in 2000 as a decentralized administrative unit within the Federal Department of Foreign Affairs (FDFA), and was given authority by the Federal Act on the Promotion of Switzerland's image abroad. On the basis of this Act of Parliament, "Presence Switzerland supports the protection of Switzerland's interests by using various public relations tools. Its tasks include transmitting general knowledge about Switzerland, as well as a portrayal of Switzerland's diversity and attractiveness."[7]

"The permanent tasks of Switzerland's communication abroad as laid down in statute are: promoting Switzerland's visibility, explaining Switzerland's political concerns and positions to a foreign public and developing and fostering Switzerland's network of contacts with foreign decision-makers and opinion leaders abroad." It is also responsible for the management of Switzerland's participation in major international events such as World Expos and Olympic Games, and the monitoring of threats to Switzerland's image or crises affecting its image.[8]

The Cultural Foreign Policy Centre (CFPC) merged with Presence Switzerland under the latter's name in the FDFA General Secretariat in June 2012.

---

[7] www.eda.admin.ch/eda/en/home/dfa/orgcha/gensec/prs.html

[8] www.eda.admin.ch/etc/medialib/downloads/edazen/dfa/orgcha/prsdoc.Par.0038.File.tmp/Brief%20history_PRS.pdf

Presence Switzerland has a strategy on communication abroad for 2012–2015 with several objectives focusing on Switzerland's challenges and strengths (its primary thematic approach) targeted at geographic priorities.

As can be seen, Presence Switzerland treats its brand image very seriously and gets involved in monitoring and image research and promotional activities. It also links to a web portal, www.swissworld.com, that provides information on all aspects of Switzerland including people, culture, leisure, geography, environment, science, education, economy, politics and history.

This case highlights the need for nations and the public sector to drive the brand at the highest level (in this case government via Act of Parliament), and to include others in its development.

Brand management, policies, and tough decisions

In the public sector, strong and purposeful brand management and guardianship inevitably requires changes in policies. I mentioned earlier in the book that immigration and investment policies influence the friendliness of a nation's image and it is true to say that in all sectors of public sector activity it is strategic policies and not tactical promotions that make the difference in building a successful brand.

For example, if a city or a country wants to become a hub for creativity and innovation, there are several characteristics that need to be in place in order to drive innovation and creativity. The principal ones are:

- diversity and depth of talent
- global mindset
- cutting-edge technology
- a large and active youth presence and culture
- existence of sub-cultures

- tolerance and freedom of expression
- strong orientation towards the arts

These are in addition to normal expected amenities such as efficiency of systems and infrastructure, good leisure, entertainment and hospitality services, and a good transportation network.

Whereas a city like New York or London would score well on most of these characteristics, some other destinations clearly would not. It is easy, for instance, to think of countries that do not allow freedom of expression, tolerance of all people, and an active youth culture. Should they wish to become a creative hub then it would be extremely difficult, if not impossible to do so. I know of at least one country that is facing this dilemma, but is not willing to change certain policies.

Government policies are required in order to build or maintain a powerful and competitive brand, and depending on the strategic national objectives, the appropriate policies required must be researched, analysed for acceptability, and implemented. These can be tough decisions to make, and for some countries, potentially risky ones.

Another example of a tough decision made by government in order to maintain a strong brand identity and image is that of New Zealand, whose government turned down an economic opportunity in favour of its brand image.

CASE STUDY: The 100% Pure New Zealand Brand

New Zealand has just fewer than 4.5 million people and apparently around seven times as many sheep. People don't want to visit sheep, and apart from dairy products, the Maori race and rugby, some might argue that New Zealand's image conjures up little in the way of irresistible attractions, although it does have a beautiful landscape. Described by some as geographically disadvantaged due to it being close to the bottom of the earth, branding New Zealand might appear challenging; however, an interesting brand strategy has been created.

TNZ – the agency that replaced the New Zealand Tourism Board in 1999 – was charged with the task of positioning the country internationally, and the first step was to carry out some specific target-oriented market research prior to vision formulation.

The research found that several segments were attracted to New Zealand, and certain key brand strengths were:

- warm, friendly and welcoming people
- contrasting landscapes
- a feeling of space and freedom
- fresh, clean and pure
- a sense of nature and adventure

Some brand weaknesses included:

- a lack of a distinctive culture
- limited nightlife and shopping
- a bit "boring"

The basic platform for the brand was crystallized as "New Pacific Freedom," from which came the summary tagline "100% Pure New Zealand." Of course, nothing is 100 per cent pure, but this was the major communications message put out by New Zealand as a summary of all that the brand stood for.

A number of ways of expressing this were used to communicate the brand platform in advertisements including "100% Romance" and "Feel 100% in Five Days." Despite these different campaign slogans, the brand messaging never stepped away from the theme of 100 per cent

(continued)

and purity, and always showed the authenticity that New Zealand was felt to possess in respect of this.

One of the threats to the New Zealand brand strategy has come from genetically-engineered foods. The potential for genetically-created food innovations to destroy the "100% Pure" promise was, and still is, significant and possibly unavoidable unless legislation prevails against them.

This possibility was of serious concern to New Zealand and resulted in the Green Party asking the tourism industry to back its campaign to keep New Zealand free from genetic engineering. A Ministry of Environment Report concluded that "If New Zealand were to damage its clean green image, it would have a huge effect on our economy ... we must be genetically-engineered free to be 100% pure."

This is an example of strong brand management action. Whether it will be strong enough in the future remains to be seen, but this case shows that even economic opportunities can potentially damage a brand. It also shows that swift action is required to neutralize any threats to the promise and the image of the brand. As of 2012, the New Zealand government still does not allow the growth of genetically-modified foods in the country but has given some approvals for the import of safe products of this kind. Some arguments for and against can be found in The New Zealand Herald, 12 September 2012, entitled "Should NZ grow genetically-modified crops?" This issue is constantly in the news and the arguments continue to receive a lot of media coverage.

This case, where the brand identity and image were chosen over economic, trade and job opportunities, demonstrates that sometimes tough policy decisions have to be taken. It also reminds us that there are many stakeholders that need to be involved and consulted in the process of taking such decisions and that transparency of discussion is important to get buy-in and commitment to such a decision. Finally, it emphasizes that strong brand management needs consistency across policies, behaviour and communications.

Brand management and the need for consistency

Great brands are built on consistency, and it is an important role for any person or brand management body to ensure that the brand remains consistent over time in all that it does. Brands are like people, in so much as if their behaviour keeps changing or is not consistent, then consumers become uneasy and lose trust.

One of the most inconsistent ways of behaviour that can lose enormous trust and customers, is by brands not sticking to their values. Authenticity, reputation and heritage have a large part to play in this, and any damage may be difficult and take time to recover from, especially if the media reports are adverse in nature.

For example, the Co-operative Group has always been an ethical organization with a reputation for transparency, openness and honesty. It is over 150 years old, has won many corporate social responsibility (CSR) awards, and brought Fairtrade to the UK. It has always been one of the most trusted brands in the retail marketplace and as a membership-based entity has always carried out a consensus process of communication and engagement. In 2013, it pulled out of a deal to buy 632 Lloyds Banking Group branches and a few months later a £1.5 billion black hole was uncovered in the Co-op's banking arm and there was a scandal involving its former chairman, Paul Flowers. "The rescue deal that was then required to save the bank led to 70% of the business being sold to private investors, calling into question its mutual and ethical status." Euan Sutherland, the group's chief executive told the BBC that it was a chance to move on from a dismal 2013, stating that "It was perhaps the worst year in our 150-year overall history."[9]

---

[9] BBC News, "Co-op boss says 2013 worst in mutual's history", 17 February 2014, www.bbc.co.uk/news/business-26223559.

As a result of this apparent disaster, which is likely to take some considerable time to play out, the Co-op Group is undertaking a nationwide poll to ask people for their views on its future. The important point to note here is that it is not just asking its members, but the general public as well, prompting *Marketing* magazine to ask, "Does the Co-op really care about what the public thinks – or is it just a PR stunt?"[10] The answer, according to this article, is that the Co-op is genuine and honest in what it is doing, and "full of intent to be better, more open, more in-tune and more-in-step." However, there is little doubt that the Co-op will need to work hard to gain the respect and trust that it had before 2013. This is especially true as it has had to take steps to remedy its financial woes and sell off other businesses, such as its farms' division and possibly its pharmacy chain, with the job losses that will inevitably ensue. This is likely to be a harder public relations task as only one month after admitting to a disastrous year, the Co-op Group has announced increases in pay and bonuses for its senior executives including the bank (which as mentioned previously, had a £1.5 billion black hole in its finances in 2013). Swiftly following on from this statement, the recently-appointed Chairman of the Group offered his resignation saying that the Co-op was "ungovernable" after leaks about the pay issue. This whole unsavoury situation led to a media and membership outcry, with statements such as, "In truth, Co-op had already lost its position as Britain's ethical bank in the eyes of consumers. Its approach to investments may still be ethical but its own behaviour long ago veered far from the principles of its founding fathers."[11]

Charities have also been on the receiving end of media angst lately, accused of bullying people over the telephone in their search for

---

[10] Jones, Kate, " Does the Co-op really care about what the public thinks - or is it just a PR stunt?", *Marketing Magazine*, 18 February 2014, www.marketingmagazine.co.uk/article/1281368/does-co-op-really-care-public-thinks—just-pr-stunt

[11] Griffiths, Ben, "Sutherland looks over-sensitive and like he's losing control at crisis-stricken Co-op", 11 March 2014, www.dailymail.co.uk/money/news/article-2577806/Co-op-boss-Euan-Sutherland-takes-Facebook-blast-board-members-leaking-information-3-6m-pay-deal-company-comes-fire-for.html

donations. Evidently, complaints about charity hotlines have risen three-fold from 2012, according to the Fundraising Standards Board watch-dog, who cited the hotline's tone, frequency, and the way in which phone numbers have been obtained. This type of aggressive fundrais-ing is "increasingly being adopted on behalf of major charities including UNICEF, the NSPCC, the RNIB, Barnado's, Scope and The Children's Society."[12] Hounding tactics causing people much distress were high-lighted in this article with more examples involving Amnesty Interna-tional and other charities.

Activities like those mentioned above that often go directly against the brand and organizational values are not the way to build trusted brands, and instead much damage can be done to the brand image. The advent of social media and the emergence and protection of "whistle-blowers" mean that however good brand management is in general, it only takes one issue to slip through the net and unfortunate conse-quences can occur.

Summary

- Brand management skill is essential to the success of any public sector brand. It is of little use having a good brand strategy if it is not imple-mented and managed well.
- Brand management involves trying to control everything a brand says and does, but sometimes the elements that affect a brand's image are not possible to control. In formulating, implementing and managing any brand strategy, all stakeholders should be involved whenever possible as without inclusiveness, buy-in and commitment, optimum success is unlikely, and in some cases intra-brand competition may be a result.

---

[12] Rawstorne, Tom, "How giving to charity can trigger MONTHS of bullying calls to your home", 3 March 2014, www.dailymail.co.uk/news/article-2571771/How-giving-charity-trigger-MONTHS-bullying-calls-home.html

- The most effective way to manage a brand and minimize under-performance is to set up a structure to ensure that discipline is introduced into the brand management process otherwise the brand will evolve in an ad hoc manner. For public sector brands, a two-tier structure is recommended with strategic priorities and decisions being set and taken by a senior body of ministers or executives forming a Brand Management Council (BMC) and a Brand Working Committee (BWC), whose task it is to produce ideas for enhancing the brand across all functions and levels, and ensuring that activities commissioned by the BMC are implemented in the best possible ways.
- Looking at brand touchpoints where the consumer comes into contact with the brand is a good way to measure how well the brand is doing compared to competitors.
- Public sector brand managers need to be aware that building brand trust and loyalty is less about advertising and more about policies, even though these are part of the marketing mix. They should be aware that sometimes policy decisions have to be taken that may lose certain opportunities but will generate brand consistency that will prove to be better in the long run. Staying true to the brand's values and what it stands for is probably the most important aspect of brand management.

In the next chapter I will look at public sector brand communication strategy and how this fits into the management and implementation of public sector brands.

Chapter 7

Brand Communications Strategy

One of the most commonly-used parts of the public sector brand implementation and management activities is communications, which can take many forms and be both strategic and tactical in nature.

Brand communications is particularly important as it seeks to impart the key messages of the brand internally and externally and if not carefully constructed can be very inconsistent at times. Over-emphasizing communications and the wrong choice of channels can sometimes lead to intra-brand competition.

There are numerous areas of communications that need to be addressed when implementing a brand strategy for a public sector organization, and tactically these can include advertising, promotion, design and visual identity, physical outlets, the Internet, and public relations. However, before diving in to use any communications channels, the first and foremost task is to develop a communications strategy using the brand strategy.

What is a brand communications strategy?

A brand communications strategy is a comprehensive blueprint document that is used to drive all communications initiatives at every touchpoint the brand has with its target audiences. Essentially it demonstrates how the brand vision, personality and positioning statements can be most effectively and memorably communicated, and it identifies the best possible approaches in communicating key messages to those audiences. This means it must elicit key messages from the brand and direct them in a manner tailored to various target audiences. In other words, it should be capable of delivering over-arching master brand messages and also targeted and relevant sub-positioning messages for different target audiences.

A communications strategy reminds all involved in brand communications, including outside agencies used by the organization, of three things:

- How we want the target audience(s) to think and feel about the brand.
- How we can get them to believe in the brand.
- How a stronger belief in the brand will result in increased brand preference and loyalty.

Further objectives arising from a brand communications strategy include ensuring that all communications initiatives are consistent in look, feel, tone and manner, and that there is no budget wastage emanating from non-effective, non-relevant messaging or personal preference.

Communications objectives

As with any strategy it is important that key objectives are articulated that can either be qualitative or quantitative in nature, for example:

- To increase brand top-of-mind awareness from 30 per cent to 50 per cent in one year.
- To create awareness and educate customers on the latest service.

Target audience profiles are normally built with care, on the basis of research such as that undertaken by Australia in discovering the needs and wants of a segmented audience called "Experience Seekers" as described in Chapter 5. There are many ways of discovering different target audiences, for example, they could be defined by:

- Affinity groups, such as NGOs, journalists, environmentalists, activists.
- Demographical factors, such as income, age, or family lifestyle.
- Geographic factors, such as regions or areas of population density.
- Psychographic elements, such as social class and lifestyle.

Whatever means are used, it is important to develop a brand communications strategy that is capable of addressing all constituencies.

Figure 7.1 below shows the link between brand strategy, communications strategy and the means of communicating the messages.

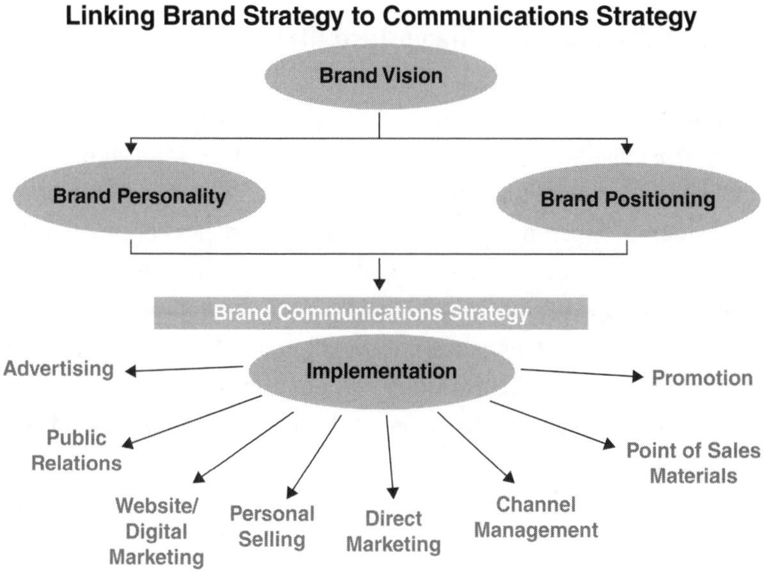

Linking Brand Strategy to Communications Strategy

Figure 7.1 Linking Brand Strategy to Communications Strategy.

The need for consistency

The key to success in brand communications is to develop a strategy with specific objectives and ensure that key messages are developed and applied consistently across all communications channels. The key messages are derived from the brand vision and positioning; the look, feel, tone and manner of how these are communicated, are driven by the personality traits. For example, if a brand personality is based around 'warmth' and 'friendliness', then all communications should reflect this whether via advertisements, promotional events, the website or other electronic channels and so on. Or if 'innovative' and 'entrepreneurial' are two main characteristics then all communications should in themselves be seen to be executed in innovative ways.

We can see how brand strategy is converted into holistic communications in practice by looking at the Building Brand Australia case below.

CASE STUDY: Building Brand Australia[1]

Introduction
Brand Australia has always been at the forefront of tourism branding and in the course of its life from its creation in 1995 to today, the brand has not only helped position Australia as a world-class destination for holiday visitors, but has also helped build the awareness of trade and investment opportunities in the country at the same time.

In order to further enhance the overall Brand Australia offering, an initiative called Australia Unlimited was put in place to build a broader brand for the country and cover trade, investment, education and other sectors.

---

[1] This case is taken from www.tourism.australia.com/about-us/brand-australia.aspx. Reproduced with permission of Tourism Australia (www.tourism.australia.com)

This case study covers both the tourism and non-tourism aspects of Brand Australia, and this is the way in which I expect many countries to follow. Tourism has always been relatively easy for countries to brand as the unique features and cultures they offer, lend themselves to differentiation. The global market has been well researched and segmented, but in the current highly-competitive world that covers many other sectors, the techniques of branding are now being used to promote the other capabilities and opportunities that countries have to offer.

The first part of the case illustrates how Brand Australia was developed for the tourism industry and linked to brand communications.

Brand Australia objectives

The Tourism Australia Act (2004) passed by the Australian Government has been the basis for all brand development since that time, and its objectives were stated to be:

- To influence people to travel to Australia, including for events;
- To influence people travelling to Australia to also travel throughout Australia;
- To influence Australians to travel throughout Australia, including for events;
- To help foster a sustainable tourism industry in Australia; and
- To help increase the economic benefits to Australia from tourism.

A Tourism Australia's Outcome Statement for 2013/14 was approved by the Government and added to this by stating that the main goal was to "Increase demand for Australia as a destination, strengthen the travel distribution system and contribute to the development of a sustainable tourism industry through consumer marketing, trade development and research activities."

(continued)

Brand Australia positioning, proposition and personality

The way in which the brand has been constructed is to make the positioning statement the key driver for all brand communications, and as is the case with all positioning statements, it defines why the brand is different and better. Positioning statements may be written in different formats but essentially they always have this aim in mind. For Brand Australia, the statement reads:

"The people of Australia are friendly and straight talking and open. Their sense of mateship and their no worries attitude make all visitors feel welcome. They make it easy to enjoy adventures beyond imagination. Whether it's in Australia's wide-open landscapes, pristine oceans or vibrant cities a holiday in Australia is an opportunity to experience a vast yet accessible adventure playground. You don't just visit Australia, you live it."

Brand Australia distils this statement into a brand proposition that is the key message that describes what makes the brand a unique holiday destination and captures the sense of what a visitor can expect to experience on a trip to Australia. This proposition states that:

"On holiday in Australia you don't switch off you switch on. The unique experiences you have and the people you meet will make you feel uplifted and full of life."

To complete the brand strategy there is a brand personality that determines the unique human characteristics associated with the brand. As with most good brand attributes, the brand personality is created using traits that are emotional in nature, and they are used to communicate in every way – look, feel, attitude, tone and manner relate to how the brand is communicated to the target audience. Brand Australia has four main personality characteristics, which are:

- high spirited
- down to earth
- irreverent
- welcoming

With the objectives and strategy in place, the key messages are then defined that will ensure that creative execution in whatever form will be consistent in what it says to the various target audiences.

Tourism Australia's five key brand messages

From the brand positioning, proposition and personality statements and definitions, the five key messages for Brand Australia were derived. These are detailed below as per the information on the Brand Australia website, and it demonstrates the fact that once the key messages are derived from the strategy and clearly defined there is no doubt as to what the creative execution should focus on.

Key Message 1. Transformation: A holiday to Australia would give me a fresh perspective

Australia is a place that changes you. You arrive with all the stresses and pressures of modern-day life, but while you're here, the land and the locals very quickly begin to wash away all those unwanted feelings and leave you feeling uplifted, energized and reconnected with your friends or family.

Key Message 2. Immersion: Holidays in Australia are about participating in life, not observing it

Getting involved is a way of life in Australia. We don't sit back and watch things pass us by. That's why holiday experiences here create such amazing memories. You'll leave with stories that will last a lifetime, about how Steve the lifesaver taught you to surf your first wave on Bondi Beach or Bill the winemaker let you pick grapes in his vineyard in the Barossa.

Key Message 3. Adventure: Australia is an adventure holiday destination

Spend some time here and it won't take you long to realize that Australia is an "outdoors" country. Whether you want to hike through

(continued)

the Kimberley or learn to surf on the Gold Coast, Australia offers an activity for everyone. The vastness of the land offers different kinds of adventures everywhere you turn, and it's the kind of place that encourages you to "give it a go."

Key Message 4. Nature: Australia offers involving experiences in the natural environment

It is a vast land, full of stunning natural landscapes and some of the most unique and friendly forms of wildlife on the planet. Whether it be the remoteness of outback Australia, the pristine waters of the Sunshine Coast or the amazing wildlife of the Kakadu National Park, it won't take long to clear the mind of the hustle and bustle of modern day city life.

Key Message 5. Welcoming: Australia is a welcoming holiday destination

Australian people are some of the friendliest people on earth. From the moment you arrive, it doesn't take long to feel like you belong here. Mateship is what we're famous for and no matter where you go or what you do you'll always feel welcome.[2]

These five key messages are used in all forms of brand communications, and it is important that they are done so in a very consistent manner. In order to ensure consistency, brand managers not only have to use these messages to brief the advertising, public relations, events agencies and others they work with, but they have to create consistent ways of helping everyone to understand them. In the case of Brand Australia the team has produced several helpful media guides. These include the following:

- A brand book called *"Australia, the land that tells a thousand stories."*

---

[2] *Ibid.*

This is described by Brand Australia as a brand foundations book, which was written to help partners and members of the tourism industry understand the brand concepts that underpin all of Tourism Australia's activities.

- A brand film and image gallery.

The brand film profiles Australia's extensive experience offering and has three versions, (domestic, global and instrumental), all of which can be downloaded from the Image Gallery for use by industry partners.

The extensive development of strategic brand communications as shown above must be consistently applied across all channels and yet must be updated and be made freshly relevant as time goes by and to avoid constant repetition. However, this must be done by way of evolution and not revolution as the latter can damage brand equity and confuse consumers.

The use of evolutionary brand communications campaigns

Tourism and other public sector brands are often promoted through global communication campaigns to create not just brand awareness, but to represent a call to action by encouraging people to book their next trip or take that next step to engaging with the brand. However, campaigns that are successful take one theme and keep evolving it for freshness and relevance over many years as opposed to developing totally different themes every two or three years. Singapore falls into the latter category, constantly switching themes, and this not only confuses target audiences abroad but also Singaporeans, who are a necessary part of the brand delivery. For example, one campaign of "Uniquely Singapore" was run for a few years and then changed to "Your Singapore." Changing in an abrupt and different way like this not only disrupts consumer "friendliness" with the brand, but also demands a huge amount of financial resource to produce a new range of global communications for media consumption.

For Australia the main campaign for them has been "There's nothing like Australia," the first iteration of which ran for three years. Campaigns that are run, as this one was, for a lengthy period need to be refreshed from time to time with new creative execution. According to Tourism Australia, the next phase of the campaign builds on this successful and established platform and "takes it a step further by specifically focusing on quality, highlighting examples of some of the very best attractions and experiences that Australian tourism has to offer." This extension of the communications platform was launched in May 2010 and was called "Together we can show the world why there's nothing like Australia."

To bring the brand to life through this campaign, Australians were invited to share their favourite domestic holiday destinations with the world. It was a major communications initiative and one of the country's biggest consumer-generated promotions. The response from the Australian people was substantial, and nearly 30 000 stories and photos were uploaded to www.nothinglikeaustralia.com. Tourism Australia says, "These stories now sit within an interactive, digital map of Australia, giving travellers around the world ideas and inspiration for their Australian holiday. The map also sits on www.australia.com, which draws more than a million unique visitors each month."

The "There's nothing like Australia" campaign theme was designed to be long-lasting and flexible, something which could be updated as necessary to stay relevant in a highly-competitive and fast-changing global tourism environment. So far, it has been used by 180 Tourism Australia partners including airlines, state and territory tourism organizations, travel distributors and the Australian industry.

In 2012 the campaign evolved to include a new advertising creative. As with the campaign's first phase, the creative focused strongly on the digital, social media and advocacy channels that are fundamental to vacation planning. This phase of the "There's nothing like Australia" campaign focuses more on the quality of the holiday experience, highlighting the very best of these that Australia offers.

Brand Australia also offers its stakeholders a great deal of assistance to encourage them to grow Brand Australia and grow their businesses, including tools for tourism operators, campaign concepts and examples, a print advertisement section, an interactive tablet app and hub and help in accessing Tourism Australia's fans on Facebook, as well as other campaign assistance.

Through the above means, Brand Australia has built a solid, research-based strategy with tailored communications, as well as engaging with and assisting businesses in the industry. It has demonstrated the way in which a brand can evolve over time and remain relevant to the changing needs of consumers.

Avoiding revolutionary campaign management

All brands have to manage their communications and messaging with consistency and yet keep them fresh and relevant. This is normally done by introducing campaigns that stick to the core messages but keep the execution (advertising, promotion, public relations, Internet etc.) interesting to the target audiences. This is standard practice and most public sector brands have agency assistance to help with this. However, brand managers must be vigilant and ensure that new creative execution does not go "off brand" and cause confusion or discord.

One example of communications revolution and disruption happened in New York. There was considerable media attention given to a headline by the *Toronto Star* on 1 June 2012, which read, "'I love NY' logo is dropping its iconic heart." The article went on to say that the logo was being rein-vented, and the heart symbol replaced with images such as a pizza slice, a lighthouse, and a roller coaster as part of a USD5 million advertising cam-paign. The article went on to explain, "For the first time since the logo's creation nearly 40 years ago, the public is being asked to help remake the 'I love NY' logo by submitting personal sketches that illustrate what they love about the state." New York Governor, Andrew Cuomo, was quoted as saying, "This campaign reinvents one of our state's greatest assets – the 'I love NY' icon – which is known the world over as one of the most suc-cessful symbols ever," and that "This campaign brings that icon to life in order to highlight all of the things people love about New York." The rest of the article featured the debate about why icons such as this should or should not be changed with the advertising agency naturally defending its position. My view is that such a great asset that has global awareness should not be played around with, and although it was an attempt to engage people more, it is likely to detract from decades of brand equity and awareness that has been painstakingly built up.

Brand management is a non-stop job and involves keeping one eye on the big picture in terms of vision, but at the same time meticulously managing the day-to-day detail of all brand activities. Sometimes brand managers, in their eagerness to do something new for or with the brand, get influenced by creative ideas that can appear great but may potentially cause brand damage.

The heart in "I love NY" remains an official trademark of the state's tourism department, and brings in a considerable source of income from licensing agreements as the invitation below indicates:

"Discover the branding power of New York State!

"Our iconic, global brand, I LOVE NY, is available for license. Con-necting a product, service or event with the I LOVE NY brand can build brand recognition and sales for your organization, ultimately providing a significant return on investment.

"Created by Milton Glaser in 1977, the purpose of the I LOVE NY mark was to promote tourism to New York State. The iconic mark represents the State's 11 vacation regions, New Yorker's affinity for their home state, endless branding opportunities for merchandise and advertising campaigns, and is one of the most recognized logos of modern day.

"To learn more about the I LOVE NY licensing program including the trademarks available for license, or to complete an application to license the mark, visit our Licensing Resource Center".[3]

The online presence of this brand is another example of the ubiquity of the Internet in brand building. One of the more complex issues in brand management that is developing very fast is the issue of online communication, and how to use it and deal with it on an on-going basis by harnessing new technologies and platforms. An online brand communications strategy is now a "must have" and more detail will be explained later in this chapter.

A good example of an innovative, integrated marketing campaign is given in the next case.

Integrated, Innovative Communications: "The Best Job In The World"

Campaigns should stay true to the brand and not become brands in themselves, as mentioned above, and brands should be evolutionary rather than revolutionary, but campaigns supporting brands can indeed be both revolutionary and very innovative. One of the best examples of this that I have come across is that created by Tourism Queensland, which was "The Best Job in the World" campaign. This not only demonstrated real creativity, but gained amazing results through an integrated marketing approach. It also showed how a public sector brand can take strategy and research through to implementation.

(continued)

---

[3] www.Iloveny.com

Tourism Queensland linked its brand to the master brand of Australia with a brand tag line of "Queensland – Where Australia Shines." It also used the target segmentation referred to in Chapter 5 focusing on Global Experience Seekers, in particular "connectors" and "social fun-seekers" that were found to make up over the half percentage of consumers that visit Queensland.

In the global recession at that time (2009), with a saturated tourism market, the challenge was for the brand to reach out to more people. Get more visitors, and generate more brand awareness of the 600 islands that Queensland has instead of just being know for the Great Barrier Reef.

The big creative idea was to offer "The Best Job in the World", a six-month assignment to become a Great Barrier Reef Island caretaker, cleaning the pool, feeding the fish and collecting the mail. While looking after the island the successful applicant was also expected to explore other islands and write a weekly blog reporting on the adventures. Compensation included round trip travel from anywhere in the world, room and board, all expenses while in Queensland, with a total package of AUD$150,000.[4] Anyone in the world could apply.

Some interesting facts include the budget, which was only US$1.2 million, and the use of integrated media. As well as offline and online advertisements and mobile marketing, there was coverage gained on CNN, ESPN Sports and even Oprah. Incredibly, the BBC produced a one hour television documentary on the campaign. Social media were used extensively to great effect. The estimated value of global publicity created was US$200 million[5], the campaign reached a global audience with 34,684 entrants from 201 countries[6], and it won three awards at the Cannes International Advertising festival in 2009. And the bottom line was a tourism increase of 20 per cent. Not a bad return on brand investment!

---

[4] http://strongerhead.com/wp-content/uploads/2012/10/DSMM-IMC-project-Best-job-in-the-world-ref-2.pdf

[5] http://en.wikipedia.org/wiki/The_Best_Job_In_The_World

[6] http://www.youtube.com/watch?v=SI-rsong4xs

The need for an online communications strategy

The increasing development and use of the Internet and the corresponding rise of other new media, especially social media, have had a major impact on branding in the public sector, especially regarding risk management and crisis communications. Global boundaries have disappeared and everyone can now be a reporter and commentator, which can be helpful or unhelpful to governments and public sector organizations. Certainly there is a strong need for any public sector brand to develop a robust online brand communications strategy, which has to be capable of working on a 24-7-365 basis.

The advent of social media has provided many challenges for both the public and the private sectors. Companies such as Facebook, which has over 1.3 billion active monthly users as at 1 January 2014,[7] have turned traditional brand communication on its head. Brand managers now have to understand that they can no longer rely on one-way communication such as advertising to talk to customers, and that they are not invited into the conversations that people are having with their friends on social media sites.

The issue here is that social media provide platforms for people to talk about brands and say what they think and feel about them, without the brand owners and managers necessarily knowing what has been said. Brand owners are therefore potentially less able to influence consumers now than they used to be, although recently developed analytical methods can reveal how many times a brand is mentioned, some indications of content, and where brand-related conversations are taking place via, for example, heat maps and other metrics. Brand managers have to find ways of communicating with people on social media platforms in real time, along with blogs, YouTube, Twitter and other vehicles. That said, it is of little use for public sector brands to use social media by merely establishing a presence in order to push out their own messages. People and communities that use social media are very sensitive to this

---

[7] www.statisticbrain.com/facebook-statistics/

kind of communications, and if they sense a lack of authenticity this will be picked up quickly and shared with their friends and colleagues.

For the public sector this can be very problematic. In an instant, anything a government says or does, or any activity that people feel unhappy about with any public sector institution or organization, can literally travel around the world in seconds. As an example, as of 1 January 2014, the number of active, registered Twitter users was 645 750 000 activating 1 billion tweets every five days (9100 per second).[8] The bad news is that a public sector brand image can take a battering very quickly, which may take some time to recover from.

However, social media is increasingly being used in a proactive way by national and local governments, states, cities and other public sector institutions for a variety of purposes.

For example, events that require immediate action such as a natural disaster or other crises, can be alerted to government agencies that can respond much more quickly than ever before, as demonstrated with the Hurricane Sandy response updates on Facebook. It is fast, and can be used for disaster preparedness and response. When an earthquake shook the northeast of the USA in 2011, many New Yorkers were informed of it via Twitter before shaking actually started. Social media allows for real time two-way conversations with everyone having a voice, is transparent, and is an efficient way of communicating. Much has been written about the impact of social media on risk and crisis communications, and in particular how it can be a beneficial tool, but also about how it can create challenges for crisis managers. An OECD working paper[9] provides a good insight and summary of this, with case examples, illustrating the different practices used by the public sector in preparing for and handling emergencies and crises.

---

[8] www.statisticbrain.com/twitter-statistics/

[9] Wendling, C., Radisch, J. and Jacobzone, S., "The Use of Social Media in Risk and Crisis Communication", *OECD Working Papers on Public Governance*, No. 25, OECD Publishing, 2013, doi: 10.1787/5k3v01fskp9s-en

Social media can also be used for forecasting results in voting, as shown during the 2012 USA presidential election, when Twitter developed a new political analysis tool, Twindex, to gauge online conversations and public sentiment for candidates. It can be used to build brands, as New York did when it created 280 social profiles to become one of the most connected cities worldwide, connecting people to many public services that affected their lives.[10]

Regarding metrics and measuring results, there are 10 basic metrics organized into seven main categories that government agencies can analyse through social media platforms:[11]

- Breadth (community size and growth).
- Depth (conversions and viewing).
- Direct Engagement (engagement volume and responsiveness).
- Loyalty (return community).
- Customer Experience (sentiment, indicators, survey feedback).
- Campaigns.
- Strategic Outcomes.

Non-profits

Things are changing rapidly in the digital world. For example, a Weber Shandwick Social Impact survey of non-profits in 2009 found that 88 per cent experimented with social media but struggled to demonstrate its value to their organizations.[12] However, this situation is now reversing as non-profits realize the opportunities that can be gained by using social media. Alec Stern, a strategic market development expert, says that when used well, marketing

---

[10] For these and other examples see http://mpadegree.org/social-media-use-by-the-government/

[11] For examples of these categories see www.howto.gov/social-media/using-social-media-in-government/metrics-for-federal-agencies

[12] KRC Research, "Weber Shandwick Social Impact Survey Finds 88% of Nonprofits Experimenting with Social Media While Struggling to Demonstrate its Value to their Organizations", 13 November 2009, www.krcresearch.com/news_socialImpact.html

using social media helps source new members, volunteers or donors for non-profit organizations. The important learning point here is that key target audiences should have great experiences and feel content, which can then be used to drive social visibility. Stern says, "Great content and experiences make people feel connected to an organization, and when these connections happen on places like Facebook, Twitter, and LinkedIn, one-to-one conversations turn into socially visible endorsements for an association or non-profit."[13]

This view is empirically endorsed by MDG Advertising, which says that social giving is thriving as a means for non-profits seeking donations. In a 2012 survey on social giving, it found the following interesting results:

"Facebook is favoured by 98 per cent of non-profits, followed by Twitter trusted by 74 per cent, YouTube utilized by 66 per cent..."

As well as individual giving via these platforms, which is increasing every year, people influence their friends to donate "leading 68 per cent of their contacts to learn more about the foundation and 39 per cent to give to that charity... with Twitter mentions yielding up to 10 times more money."[14]

MDG says that another of the features of the online social media revolution is crowdfunding with over 500 platforms worldwide The amounts of money raised is illustrated by the fact that there has been a 91 per cent increase in the sum of funds collected in 2012 over last year. Clearly, the rapid rate of growth of social giving is changing the face and future of charitable donations.

The conclusion from this and other studies makes it clear there is no doubt that all public sector brands will be turning more to online strategies to build awareness, members and funding. Indeed, according to

---

[13] Stern, Alec, "Engage, Inform, Recruit: How Nonprofits Can Use Social Media to Recruit Donors and Volunteers", 5 December 2013, www.nten.org/articles/2013/engage-inform-recruit-how-nonprofits-can-use-social-media-to-recruit-donors-and-volunteers-0

[14] MDG Blog, "2012: It Was a Very Good Year for Social Giving", 11 December 2012, www.mdgadvertising.com/blog/2012-it-was-a-very-good-year-for-social-giving/

MDG, social media is a prime driver for tourism and destination branding, as in another study it says, "Social media networks are prime destinations for finding views on venues... This talk drives so much traffic to websites that travel marketers and their branding firms need to use these social media networks to boost their bookings and business."[15]

So what we have learnt in recent years is that not only is brand communication moving away from the one-way traditional path towards a two-way conversation with much more involvement from the consumer, but also that people, through technology advancement, are able to almost instantly share their perceptions of brands with hundreds of thousands of others and thus influence brand image enormously. In addition, they expect brands to engage with them in their own preferred way of carrying out a conversation in their preferred time, just as they do with their friends. This is causing brand managers to completely re-think their communications and engagement strategies and is forcing them to adopt a more democratic approach to brand management.

In the digital world everything is converging and according to many technology and brand experts, the future of consumer interaction with both private and public sector brands will be through mobile connections. This convergence to the predominant use of mobile technology is already happening and as a result, mobile applications (apps) represent another opportunity for interactive brand communications and are currently being used at both organizational and national levels.

Mobile apps

The mobile internet world has been taken up very quickly by the public sector, and the use of apps is spreading rapidly. Denmark claims to be the

---

[15] MDG Blog, How Social Media Networks are the Ticket to Driving Travel and Hospitality Bookings", 5 February 2014, www.mdgadvertising.com/blog/using-social-networks-to-influence-travel-and-hospitality-bookings-infographic/

first country to develop a smart phone app that is aimed at journalists and media, but in reality will surely be useful and attractive for potential tourists and investors.

The app, "Denmark Stay Tuned" is funded by the Danish Government and embedded in The Ministry of Foreign Affairs of Denmark. It is free and provides users with texts, images and videos as well as local contacts and aims to introduce you to:

"... the happiest people in the world ... the new Nordic cuisine, classic and contemporary design, world-class Danish architecture and how Danes think out of the box in many different ways. Finally you will get a rundown of national quirks and the oddest things quintessentially Danish."[16]

We are likely to see mobile applications used more and more by public sector brands as new mobile tools and platforms emerge for people all over the world to use and as the global growth of mobile phone sales continues to soar. However, as traditional methods of reaching customers continue to diminish while online interactions increase, there is still room for the personal touch.

Direct sales and promotion in public sector brand communications

Public sector entities sometimes use normal communications channels such as advertising and direct interaction with the public to raise awareness and interest. Most tourism, trade and investment boards do this by attending promotional fairs such as Expos and other major events

---

[16] Andersen, Hans Christian,"Stay Tuned - free app about Denmark", 15 June 2012, www.visitdenmark.com/denmark/stay-tuned-free-app-about-denmark

of relevance, and by working through third-party event organizers. Most ministries or statutory boards in these three areas of activity have offices in different countries where they can meet their target audiences on a face-to-face basis. Others have representation in embassies and high commissions.

Few public sector brands have adopted the model used by non-profit organization, Oxfam, who has branches and shops in over 90 countries selling used products of various kinds donated by supporters. Recently, Oxfam has stepped further into retail marketing with the introduction of online shopping and upmarket boutiques. The case below focuses mainly on Oxfam's physical presence, but it must be said that, as is the case with Oxfam, all public sector brands must have an online presence.

CASE STUDY: Oxfam's Retail Boutiques and Online Shopping

An interesting recent development for the Oxfam brand is to move into the more upmarket retail stream and introduce a chain of boutiques in the UK. Oxfam hopes to capitalize on the designer items that it receives from donations and so appeal to a wider audience willing to pay higher prices for premium and luxury goods. According to Oxfam its boutiques "create a new benchmark for sustainable fashion. They provide shoppers with a unique style, beautiful one-off clothes, and the assurance that every item will raise money to fight poverty around the world."

Oxfam has even segmented these into five categories, which are:

- Loved for Longer: An ever-changing range of unique clothes and accessories.
- Fair Trade: Great fashion can put people first.
- Reinvented: An exclusive range of one-offs created for Oxfam.

(continued)

- Made with Love: Unique pieces to treasure made by talented volunteers.
- Good Fashion Sense: Clothes and accessories designed to make a difference.

It goes on to say, "You can also buy great Loved for Longer Men's and Women's clothing on the Online Shop, as well as beautiful Fair Trade and Good Fashion Sense jewellery from the Ethical Collection."[17]

The reasoning behind the upmarket move by Oxfam is partly inspired by analysis of the stock they receive from donors and the potential to sell the goods on at higher prices in a better environment; and offering goods from all the fashion and luxury brands that people cannot afford to buy new. This idea was backed by consumer research that revealed a customer group that wanted "a more contemporary shopping experience." From a brand perspective, the noticeable thing about this retail initiative is that it is always tied back to the brand to remind people of what Oxfam stands for. As Oxfam's chief executive Barbara Stocking says, "Our boutiques will provide shoppers with beautiful clothes in a sophisticated environment – with the assurance that they are both sustainable and help Oxfam to tackle poverty."

By opening boutiques, Oxfam has thus reversed its traditional ways of operating in terms of revenue generation, but has managed the brand in a very consistent way. One of the lessons from private sector global brand management is that consistency over time is vital in communicating with consumers and reaching out to potential customers and supporters. It is very important not to step away from what the brand stands for and if any new initiative does not fit with the brand strategy, it is best not to embark on it.

Life is tough in the retail environment these days and in addition to the new boutiques to be opened, Oxfam is revamping its 700 UK

---

[17] www.oxfam.org.uk/shop/local-shops/oxfam-boutiques

stores and launching a new television campaign to boost falling sales. Trials in 35 renovated stores produced a double-digit increase in sales, but Oxfam also found that customer numbers increased as they had better access and this together with better product display, enhanced employee motivation. These positive findings gave Oxfam the confidence to carry out this major brand outlet rejuvenation programme.

The brand communications also changed with the new advertising, and instead of generating advertisements that showed extreme poverty and suffering, Oxfam focused more on positive messages such as the successes achieved in disease survival rates and increased numbers of children going to school. The consumer insight behind this was that potential donors were more likely to give donations when brand communications concentrated on hope as opposed to desperation.

The example of Oxfam shows that one of the elements of real importance to the development and management of any brand is the engagement of both customers and employees. The engagement of stakeholders is the subject of Chapter 8, but another form of engagement and brand communications in the public sector is that provided by brand vectors such as sport.

Global brand vectors – sport and product placement

Brand vectors are those things that can really make a huge difference to a country or an organization's brand image if all goes well and one of the most popular is sport. Nations go to great lengths to secure the world's best sporting events, and it's not just for the fun of it. One of the brand management weapons that has an amazing impact on image is a well-orchestrated event (or series of events), and the more major the event, the more impact there is on the image and other national objectives. Sporting events have grown in importance, especially since the 1984 Los Angeles Olympic Games demonstrated for the first time that such magnificent occasions could also generate profits. Since then, major events have not proven to be merely financial one-offs, they have been used as vectors for permanent national image changes.

Both developed and developing nations are desperate to get the custody of a great sporting event. For example, Brazil has been awarded the 2014 FIFA World Cup and the 2016 Olympic Games.

Formula 1 is an annual event that is watched by billions and to be included in the "circuit" is a major achievement and a showcase for the national image. Malaysia constructed a beautiful new track at Sepang with no expense spared to get on the list. China, Abu Dhabi and Bahrain all compete in this huge entertainment business. Even stalwarts like Monaco, where Formula 1 has been held since 1929, are spending enormous sums to keep their place. Prince Albert, when asked about the contribution of Formula 1 to Monaco in the annual parade of world sporting events on a scale of 1–10, gave it a score of 15! Nations benefit hugely from sporting events.

The Olympic Games is probably the biggest spectacle and can be good not just for communicating with a global audience, but also for engaging with citizens, boosting morale and gaining economic benefits. *The Economist* said, "The Beijing Games were intended to show off China's spending and organizational power. London's Games were a means of bringing back to life a poor part of the capital at a speed that defied normal budgets and planning regulations. Tokyo hopes the 2020 Games can gee-up Japan's lacklustre economy."[18]

Research following the Sydney Olympic Games in 2000 showed results that were just as spectacular as the Games themselves. Between 1997 and 2004 there were estimated to be 1.6 million "Olympic-induced" visitors. During the Games there were 111 000 visitors, 10 300 athletes from

---

[18] *The Economist*, "Why would anyone want to host the Olympics?", 8 September 2013, www.economist.com/blogs/economist-explains/2013/09/economist-explains-0#sthash.rgd1qMwW.dpuf

199 countries, 18 000 media people, 5100 support staff, and 3.7 billion TV viewers worldwide. But the economic benefit accruing to Australia was estimated to be $6.1 billion over the period 1997–2004, and 150 000 new jobs were created. That's a great return!

Since then, there has been a considerable amount of debate as to whether or not economic benefits can be gained from the Olympic Games but in a 2009 working paper, the National Bureau of Economic Research says, "hosting a mega-event like the Olympics has a positive impact on national exports. This effect is statistically robust, permanent, and large; trade is around 30 per cent higher for countries that have hosted the Olympics. Interestingly however, we also find that unsuccessful bids to host the Olympics have a similar positive impact on exports. We conclude that the Olympic effect on trade is attributable to the signal a country sends when bidding to host the games, rather than the act of actually holding a mega-event. We develop a political economy model that formalizes this idea, and derives the conditions under which a signal like this is used by countries wishing to liberalize."[19] It appears then that merely being associated with this stellar event can boost tangible and non-tangible benefits, sending signals that have an impact on image.

There is still some dispute as to how much the UK benefited economically from the 2012 Games, and the government was quoted as stating that, "The UK economy has seen a £9.9 billion boost in trade and investment from hosting the 2012 London Olympic and Paralympic Games, research suggests."[20] Whether this was offset by costs or what the legacy will be, is still a subject for debate. What is indisputable though is that holding the 2012 Games worked wonders for UK morale in a time of economic austerity and facilitated a great deal of investment and trade deals.

---

[19] Rose, Andrew K. and Spiegel, Mark M., *"The Olympic Effect"*, NBER Working Paper No. 14854, Issued in April 2009, www.nber.org/papers/w14854

[20] BBC News, "London 2012 Olympics have boosted UK economy by £9.9bn", 19 July 2013, www.bbc.co.uk/news/uk-23370270

It also showed Britain off at its best on the global stage and this internal and external brand-related effect is what it is really all about.

Another great example of sport-related multi-brand benefits can be seen with Yorkshire and its involvement in the 2014 Tour de France.

In what has been regarded as a major coup in the world of branded sports events, Yorkshire managed to bring the 101st Tour de France (the largest annual sporting event in the world with a worldwide television audience of 3.5 billion people) to the county for the first two stages of the 2014 race, as part of the Grand Départ, that started in Leeds took in some of the county's most famous sights and landmarks.

Tour de France race director Christian Prudhomme described Yorkshire's Grand Départ as the "grandest" in the 111-year history of the race. "I can see the Tour in their hearts, and in their eyes. For that, I say thank you to everyone in Yorkshire who has made this Grand Départ so very, very special." He added "when you said you would deliver the grandest Grand Départ it was the truth, you have raised the bar for all future hosts of the Tour de France."[21]

This kind of brand initiative produces a similar outcome to that of the Nation Brand Effect I discussed in chapter three, where the major brand and sub-brands benefit from each other. Yorkshire gained global exposure not just for the benefit of its tourism industry, which will be considerable, but also for all the Yorkshire branded businesses that were involved in official sponsorship of the Tour Grande Départ. These included the Yorkshire Building Society (that painted sheep yellow in fields next to the roads of the stage), Leeds and Bradford International Airport (sponsoring a gaming app called "Tour de Yorkshire"), Sheffield Hallam University (with its branded Land Rovers backing up the pelaton), Taylor's of Harrogate (with its specially created coffee blend), Yorkshire Tea (a brand of Taylor's with its special edition tea packs of "Yorkshire Thé) and other brands. 2.5 million spectators came

---

[21] http://www.bbc.co.uk/sport/0/cycling/28188083

out onto the route to watch the tour in Yorkshire, which alone was valuable for enhancing brand awareness and engagement. Coupled with the massive TV coverage, it was a win-win for Yorkshire, its tourism and its brands.

Summary

- Communications is an important part of brand strategy implementation and must be managed properly by those responsible for overall brand management as well as those in charge of functions such as corporate communications.
- Every public sector brand requires both an online and offline communications strategy with clearly defined key messages that relate to the vision, values, personality and positioning of the brand.
- The traditional way of communicating with various groups of people such as advertising and direct sales, which tend to be one-way in nature, is slowly but surely diminishing in favour of digital methods which are, by their nature, two-way. There are exceptions where the customers require face-to-face attention and interaction, as with retail outlets.
- There are rapid increases in the use of the Internet and social media by customers and other stakeholders, public sector organizations, and anyone in the world who wishes to make comments about brand behaviour. This will continue to change the way in which brands communicate and are managed, and the public sector has to learn to communicate with many different types of audience in real time on a continuous basis. Social networking in particular provides public sector institutions with the opportunity to receive feedback by engaging in conversations and to respond in a timely manner.
- As the previous chapter and this one have illustrated, it is very difficult to control and manage brands when things go wrong and the media get involved. Dealing with adverse crisis situations and somewhat hostile comments requires fast action and transparency from brand managers.
- Major global events can help transfer the awareness and influence of public sector brands.

Chapter 8

Brand Engagement

One of the most important breakthroughs in implementing brand strategy in recent years is the attention given not just to the external customer, but to the internal customer; in other words, employees. Unless employees really understand what the brand stands for, how important it is, and how they can contribute to its success, the implementation of the brand will be limited. Buy-in and commitment from employees is critical. Often this is referred to as building a strong brand culture.

Brand engagement is essential to ensure that the customer experience is managed well and goes one step further than internal communications about the brand, by training and involving everyone in the organization to both understand and get involved with the brand. This means letting employees know how they can contribute to the development of the brand in their everyday working lives and thus involves both training and the creation of brand action plans that have to be carried out at all levels of the organization. Also involved in the brand engagement process is the analysis of brand touchpoints (where the brand comes into contact with customers) and how effective the organization is in managing the customer experience via these touchpoints.

Brand engagement is intended not just for internal employees, but for partners, communities and other stakeholders. However, it should be noted that unless the brand is well understood internally and employees align themselves in their work to the values of the brand and what it stands for, the organization will be less successful in building a strong brand experience and image for external stakeholders.

Brand engagement, corporate image, and culture

Corporate culture is a much-discussed topic these days as companies try to accommodate modern work practices and change-management styles. Many sophisticated training and organization development initiatives are implemented by internal and external specialists to suit current corporate cultures and help promote efficiency and effectiveness for the future. Corporate culture, in its crudest form, is described as "the way we do things around here". Essentially, it is the sum of a complex blend of employee attitudes, beliefs, values, rituals and behaviours that permeate a company and give it a unique style and feel.

Corporate culture can have a profound effect on both staff and customers. For staff, it can provide an invigorating, stimulating, and exciting place to work, or it can make going to work a dismal daily experience. It can empower people or enslave them. Because culture is ubiquitous, it inevitably has an impact not just inside, but also outside the organization. Customers who come into contact with staff can feel it through the morale, attitudes and expressions of the staff, and see it in the staff's comments and service standards. Corporate culture impacts considerably on corporate image, and thus has to be built and managed well.

When any organization tries to develop and maintain a good brand image, it has to create a suitable culture. For any organization wanting to build a powerful brand, that culture has to be appropriate to the essence of the brand, and so it is not surprising that using the brand and its values or personality to engage with employees and shape their behaviour, is a very positive and well-received way of creating a values-driven culture.

This approach to culture building was pioneered by the private sector, but public sector organizations are using their brand messages to inspire people and influence them to apply brand values. For example, at the start of its brand book, WWF says, "Read on to find out how you can help build on our success and make sure that our brand shines through in whatever work you're doing on behalf of the planet." It goes on to say, "The WWF brand is already internationally renowned. Together we can make it even stronger," and, "WWF is a diverse global network. But our brand unites us. By living our brand, we speak with a stronger voice and act together to help people and nature thrive."[1]

Organizations wanting to build a new corporate culture or change the existing one often do this by establishing a set of values as a behavioural guide for people to follow. The most attractive (and often most successful) way to build a brand is to create a personality for the brand – a personality that summarizes what the brand really stands for. If a brand platform is built through developing certain personality characteristics or traits, then it is easier for consumers to connect with it, and become attracted to it. Once the personality characteristics have been chosen as the building blocks of the brand, then the culture of the company can, and must, follow that same identity. WWF again shows the way in its brand book. Referring to its brand values with the acronym KODE (see Chapter 4 for the description of the values), it says, "Our values are at the heart of the way we operate and communicate. They should come across in everything we do, from speaking at a conference to answering the phone." This demonstrates the importance of engaging employees in brand building.

As every experienced brand manager knows, brand values must also be defined, explained, and implemented at every level of the

---

[1] WWF Brand Book; *One Network, One Vision, One Voice*: Published in February 2013 by WWF – World Wide Fund For Nature (Formerly World Wildlife Fund), Gland, Switzerland. Hudson, David and Jeffries, Barney/ngo.media, www.ngomedia.org.uk. Concept and Design by © ArthurSteenHorneAdamson 2011)

organization. This involves helping business units to apply the brand values strategically to everything they do by integrating the brand into business planning. It also involves integration of the brand into all departments and jobs of employees. These activities are now discussed in more detail.

Engaging employees

It is imperative that ALL employees are trained in what the brand stands for and what the brand values and personality mean, and not just in general terms. Training staff in this way not only motivates them but also gives them the answer to the question, "What does the brand mean for me, and how can I contribute in my everyday work?" Developing small, interactive brand handbooks can be used to supplement this training with fun exercises designed around the brand and its values/personality. At the end of the training staff are encouraged to write down at least three different ways in which they will change at work to become more in line with the brand and what it stands for.

It is important to remember that all employees should be involved in brand training and not just those in the front line. The "back office" people can also make a tremendous difference to the customer brand experience as they often help deliver the experience by supporting front-line activities. Brand training is good because of its all-encompassing nature and it is the "glue" that binds the employees in the organization together with shared values as shown in Figure 8.1.

A more radical way of engaging employees is by making them "owners" or "partners" in the organization, sharing the profits via dividends and bonuses. This is the model used by for-profit values-driven entities such as co-operatives and by private sector companies like the John Lewis Partnership. In the John Lewis Partnership, all staff, known as partners because they co-own the business, receive the same percentage

Bring Brand Understanding Throughout the Organization

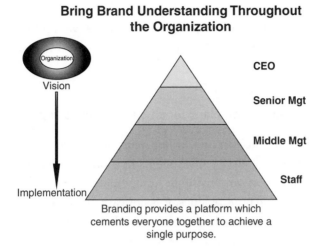

Figure 8.1 Employee Engagement through Brand Training.

of salary as a bonus; this applies from check-out assistants to the group chairman. In 2014, they announced that thanks to the 2013 results, thousands of John Lewis and Waitrose staff would "get a £2,000 bonus after Middle England's favourite retailer made more than £10 billion in sales for the first time ... all its 90 000 staff would receive bonuses worth 15 per cent of salary as they shared £202.5million, which works out at around eight weeks' pay."[2]

Co-ops (co-operatives) have historically been formed for the benefit of communities and in some cases have developed into major players in retail and other sectors. Revenues from the 300 largest co-ops total more than USD2 trillion worldwide.[3]

---

[2] "John Lewis staff cheer £2,000 bonus after record £10bn sales", 6 March 2014, www.thisismoney.co.uk/money/news/article-2575139/John-Lewis-staff-cheer-2-000-bonus.html

[3] Worth, Thibault, "Can co-ops redefine sustainable business?", 21 November 2013, www.theguardian.com/sustainable-business/cooperatives-sustainable-business-structures. This article also discusses the contribution of co-ops to sustainability and some issues of concern surrounding The Cooperative Group.

For most public sector institutions, employee engagement with the brand is the way to go and helps everyone deliver on the values; but, at different levels there has to be a deeper involvement with all departments and functions.

Develop brand action plans for all business units and functions

I have found it useful in working with both public and private sector organizations to help business units, divisions and departments produce plans for the short- and medium-term with respect to how they are going to deliver on the brand values. It is critical to include support services in this activity, as unless they also change the way in which they do things those departments impacting directly on consumers will find it difficult to implement their plans. For example, in a telecommunications company it is difficult for a marketing or sales business unit to improve performance on the value of 'friendliness' if customers receive separate bills for fixed line, mobile, Internet services and so on. Customer-friendly billing would give them just one bill covering all transactions. It is often necessary to change systems and procedures in order to provide a total impact on, and change in, consumer perceptions.

With this in mind, all divisions or departments – such as information technology, finance, research and development, human resources, production, credit control, logistics, marketing, corporate communications and others – should develop strategic and tactical action plans to demonstrate to top management how they intend to implement each brand value. These plans shouldn't contain vague statements of intent but concrete action plans detailing timing and accomplishment criteria.

Brand strategy workshops are the best way of helping departments to articulate these action plans. Once managers get used to developing such plans, the establishment of the brand is easier to achieve and control, and departments will find it easier to define people's jobs more clearly in terms of the brand.

As an example of brand strategy execution, let's take "innovation" as a key brand value or personality characteristic. We have already seen in Chapter 5 how important innovation is to the public sector. Many private sector firms have this as a brand value in their strategy, bringing it to life in different ways to ensure that products and services are truly innovative and are seen as such by consumers. Gillette is well-known for a policy of insisting that over 40 per cent of annual sales come from products introduced in the last five years; 3M has, in the past, employed a ratio of 25 per cent to help implement the same value. Kao, the Japanese personal care product company, concentrates heavily on innovation, and approximately 2000 of its 7000 employees at one stage were dedicated to research and development – around three times that of the giant Procter & Gamble. Kao's aim is to become a global player, but states it can only achieve this through producing a constant stream of new products to aggressively seize international opportunities.

The message, then, is that every brand value or personality characteristic has to be very carefully defined, not just at the corporate level but also at departmental- and job-specific levels. The brand has to live in every strategic way possible. Beyond this, the brand also has to be brought to life by every employee in the organization. In the case of larger public sector brands, there should still be an effort to bring all stakeholders into the "brand family".

At a macro-level for the public sector, culture is very important. When Liverpool became the European Capital of Culture in 2008, the whole brand was based on the city's unique culture, and it created The Liverpool Culture Company as an umbrella organization responsible for its culture programme. It also involved residents of the city in every way possible by giving many people the opportunity to be "Brand Advocates" and "Speak for Liverpool" in brand communications and campaign activities. Speak for Liverpool said on the website, "Speak for Liverpool. We're all in this together. There's space for everyone to be heard. Speak for Liverpool here."[4]

---

[4] www.liverpoolcitybrand.co.uk

Building a brand culture needs the values to permeate not just the organization but also to get buy-in and commitment to them by strategic partners and other stakeholders too.

Engaging partners and other stakeholders

Brand engagement needs to integrate external as well as internal stakeholders. For example, in the public sector, where an industry brand strategy is being built to improve its performance, the success of the formation and implementation of that strategy will depend on engaging with companies and other partners; this means that brand management, communications, and engagement must work together. The Canada Brand below is a case in point.

CASE STUDY: The Canada brand – food, glorious food!

Introduction

The following press release was placed on the website *www .brandcanada.agr.gc.ca* in 2009, describing the branding initiative associated with the Canadian food and agriculture industry.

"GOVERNMENT OF CANADA INVESTING IN CANADA BRAND MARKETING INITIATIVE

"Calgary, Alberta, September 17, 2009 – The Government of Canada is investing $32 million in the Canada Brand initiative to put the maple leaf brand on the top quality products Canadian farmers grow and increase sales around the world.

"'Canadian farmers want to make their living in the marketplace and buyers around the world are looking for the premium products the maple leaf has come to symbolize,' said Agriculture Minister Gerry Ritz. 'This investment is going to help Canadian farmers drive market research and promotional campaigns to maximize opportunities around the world.'

"The Canada Brand initiative was intended to fund market analysis, advertising campaigns and public opinion research that will promote Canada's safe, top quality agriculture.

"'By more actively promoting the strengths and benefits of the Canada Brand, the Government will be complementing the individual marketing efforts of specific agriculture and food sectors in order to open more doors and increase sales,' said Minister of National Revenue and Minister of State (Agriculture), Jean-Pierre Blackburn.

"Canada's food and agriculture is a dynamic sector clearly poised for more success. Recent market research shows that Canada already has a positive image around the world. We're known to be a trustworthy, reliable and competent people. Our land is thought of as pristine, fresh and environmentally friendly. Our food and agriculture products are considered safe, fresh, and natural.

"Branding Canada for the food and agriculture sector – Branding Canada for short – was developed in close partnership with industry and provincial governments and is based on solid research. This initiative is designed to help take Canada's strong international image and leverage it to increase the sales and profile of Canadian food and agriculture products.

"Approximately 45 per cent of Canadian domestic food and agricultural production is exported either directly as primary products or indirectly as part of processed products. In 2008 we exported $42.8 billion (Cdn) worth of food and agriculture around the world!"[5]

The Canada brand strategy

Since the above statements were issued, Agriculture and Agri-Food Canada (Agriculture et Agroalimentaire Canada) has gone on to build what is now called "The Canada Brand," with the aim of helping Canadian organizations link Canada's image more closely to their food products

(continued)

---

[5] www.brandcanada.agr.gc.ca

and gain recognition for Canadian food and agriculture products in key markets. The reason for this, according to the government department, is that while Canada has an enviable reputation as a country of clean, wide-open spaces and citizens who are honest and friendly, it is still not well-known for its food and agriculture products. It says, "We want people to instinctively decide that Canada's diverse selection of agriculture and food products will meet or exceed their experiences every time! It is well-known that a country's image can influence customer decision-making. The Canada Brand strategy builds on that positive image to help differentiate our agriculture and food products from the competition."

In building the Canada Brand strategy the main elements have been:

- a brand promise
- graphics to communicate the brand
- a unique tagline
- a photo bank
- market research
- design templates

The brand promise

This defines what the Canada Brand stands for and is described as follows. "We are committed to earning our customers' trust in Canadian agriculture and food products every day through our relentless pursuit of excellence in all that we do."

This promise was the end result of market research carried out with consumers and commercial food buyers in key export markets, which highlighted the industry attributes, in particular:

- Product excellence, linked to safety and high quality.
- Canada as a multi-cultural country, focusing on and responding to the needs of international customers.
- Commitment to continuous improvements.

- Rigorous systems in the food and agricultural industry.
- Canada's clean, pristine environment that provides good growing conditions.

Graphics, tagline, photo bank, templates and research

In communicating the brand, the visual identity includes a maple leaf, a ribbon and a tagline that says, "Quality is in our nature," all of which help to reinforce the brand promise and increase the awareness of Canada's products. A photo bank of Canadian landscapes and food products was created, and design templates to be used by companies as marketing collateral for domestic and international markets were also made available to members. In addition, Canada Brand carries out continuous market research on consumer *and buyer behaviour, again to help companies in marketing their products.*

Membership and benefits

In order to be able to use Canada Brand, companies have to become members and sign an agreement regarding terms and conditions of usage although there does not appear to be a charge for this. The main benefit for members is the opportunity to sell more products using the brand tools described above on packaging and labelling. There are also opportunities for member companies to promote themselves on a special website (*www.eatCanadian.ca*) and at promotional events.

More specifically, the Canada Brand informs potential members about the emotional and rational sides of the strategy and how that can help them. In short, they suggest that branding your product Canadian can:

- Reduce price sensitivity and command premium prices.
- Increase sales and profitability.
- Build customer loyalty based on emotions.

(continued)

- Raise the profile and value of your products.
- Help mitigate crisis when something goes wrong.

The website goes on to reiterate that being Canadian "means you're trusted and respected... a competitive edge worth building on," and that the Canada Brand uses these positive images to help build a brand to help ensure Canadian products stand out. There is further reassurance that as a member, you will be provided with in-depth assistance and advice on how to develop your branding strategy.[6]

All members of Canada's food and agriculture industry can use the brand, but in order to safeguard its value they must sign an agreement of usage and agree to certain terms and conditions.

Brand ambassadors

Although the Canada Brand communications materials do not refer specifically to the words "Brand Ambassadors" they do provide quotes from member companies. One example is by Larry McIntosh from Peak of the Market, a Canada Brand member who says, "The Canada Brand research confirmed our own analysis of certain markets and made us rethink our approach to others. I truly believe that using the Canada Brand has helped our company increase its sales." Another Canada Brand member, Scott Sigvaldason of Smart & Natural Foods Ltd said, "Having ready-made Canada Brand tools, like key messages, country research reports and a common look, gives me more time to concentrate on making contacts and networking."

Lessons from the Canada Brand

The Canada Brand is an interesting way in which to brand an industry that is of strategic importance to the country. It acts as an umbrella brand for all its members and allows them to use the brand strategy

---

[6] *Ibid.*

and tools for branding and marketing purposes. This type of initiative is especially helpful to small- and medium-sized enterprises that do not normally have the budget or the knowledge of how to develop and implement a brand strategy.

The brand uses emotional as well as rational ways of expressing the brand to its members and target markets, especially regarding trust and safety aspects, which are highly important to consumers of food and agricultural products.

The use of a "quality mark" in order to act as an endorsement by the government adds power and strength to members who use it, and serves as a means of branding the industry and the nation of Canada at the same time. This brand case study illustrates how an industry brand can leverage the impact of the Nation Brand Effect discussed in Chapter 3. As Brand Canada says, "Market research has proven that consumers associate the Canada Brand identifiers with safe, high quality products; and the more Canadian companies use the brand the more easily Canadian products will be recognized, valued and chosen!"

A visit to the site will give readers a wealth of information on how well the brand strategy has been thought through and built.[7] It really is an excellent example of building a powerful public sector brand at an industry level and how to gain buy-in and commitment from a great many customers and partners.

The use of quality marks and other public sector endorsements

Canada Brand uses a combination of words and visuals to make up its brand endorsement for its members, the words being, "Quality is in our nature." This not only helps assure end-users about the status of food

---

[7] www.marquecanadabrand.agr.gc.ca

brands they are buying that are endorsed by the government in this way, but acts in a dual capacity assuring them of good quality. This is an extremely important point for members as well as it is impossible to develop a top brand without top-class quality of its products and services.

Turkey has a similar notion with its Turquality® programme. Commenting on this programme as a part of its Top 100 Nation Brands study in 2012, BrandFinance® said:

"Turquality® was launched in 2005 to develop and promote Turkish brands. Starting initially with textiles, an area of strength for Turkey, it now covers 80+ companies and everything from industrial machinery to jewellery.

"Turquality® is not simply a branding programme but rather one that works to develop all aspects of the member companies. It helps define a strategic business plan for the companies and supports the development of executives and middle managers through a specially designed executive MBA. Further business development and market research is available through a consulting subsidy programme, where approved consulting companies' rates are supported 50 per cent by the Turkish government, allowing worldwide expertise to advise each company where and how they need it. Vision seminars with leading worldwide business leaders provide inspiration to the member companies.

"Turquality® has continued to expand the number of companies accepted into the programme from its launch, showing it is having a positive impact on both improving quality with Turkish production as well as focusing these companies on international branding. It has also spun off the Turkish design awards to showcase the very best in industrial design in 2008 and forward. These awards provide an additional highly public incentive to improve the quality of production."[8]

---

[8] "Export Brands: Turquality, Bringing Turkey's Best to the World", 1 August 2012, www.brandfinance.com/knowledge_centre/stories/export-brands-turquality-bringing-turkeys-best-to-the-world

Malaysia, too, has a National Mark of Malaysia Brand awarded to those companies who have excelled in various criteria. This includes quality assisted by a special public sector organization called SME Corp, which is a part of the Ministry of International Trade and Industry and is charged with the task of helping Malaysia's most promising small- and medium-sized businesses to develop all round capabilities including brand development.

All such initiatives are good as they encourage and help companies to grow, gain international market access and contribute to their nation's economies while acting as ambassadors for their country brands.

Summary

- Brand engagement is critical to the successful implementation of brand strategy, and communications on its own will not suffice. If at all possible, the building of the brand strategy itself should engage both internal and external stakeholders, but at the very least, as many as possible should be involved and committed to its implementation.
- From an internal perspective, training in what the brand stands for and how employees can play their part in their jobs to help make the brand outstanding is essential. A strong brand culture must prevail, and this means constant reinforcement of the vision and values. Internal communications is a part of this in addition to training. All business units, functions and departments should play their part in looking at ways in which they can make the brand come to life. Developing brand action plans is the best way in which to achieve this and motivate people.
- From an external perspective, public sector brands more than private sector brands have an obligation to find ways in which to include all stakeholders or they will find it difficult to get their brand plans to work.

When brand engagement and communications are carried out thoroughly and to a good standard, success is much more likely, and it is to the topic of tracking brand success that I now turn.

Chapter 9

Tracking Brand Success

The complexity and challenges faced are many in the implementation and management of a brand strategy. Brands are strategic assets of tremendous financial value, especially to nations and the public sector, and brand ambassadors, brand managers or brand custodians of any kind are really asset managers. With this in mind, brand management is not complete unless there is some form of tracking of the success of the brand, and this can be done in a variety of ways, all of which require some kind of market research.

The private sector has now become much more concerned with the total value of their brands, not just with profitability, and the public sector is following suit. The valuation of brands is by no means an exact science, but the sale of brands for prices far in excess of their asset valuation has meant that brand valuation has become a business in its own right. For the brand manager, this means that several measures of performance have to be taken into account simultaneously. Most research companies that evaluate brand health and performance have proprietary instruments for measuring brand equity and value, and the two concepts are different.

For instance, brand equity measurement can include a whole host of variables, which in the commercial world includes brand awareness, brand associations, brand trust and loyalty, perceived quality, price, market share and cash-flow premiums, internationality, support, protection, and many others.

The public sector also uses some of these variables in assessing brand success, depending on their nature, but in building brand equity for the public sector in general, the emphasis is focused more on values, trust, and emotional associations. With this in mind, the 'Emotional Ladder of Brand Success' as explained in Chapter 4 is particularly apt in measuring brand equity. Based on this concept, market research tools have been developed to measure the total impact of the brand on consumers, partners, or whoever else is important to the success of the brand. One such methodology is called BrandSPACE™, which takes into account the fact that the human brain has both left and right hemispheres that function differently in terms of rational and emotional activity. It is important for a brand to capture the hearts and minds of consumers and this means combining the rational dimension with the emotional dimension in the brand proposition and measuring its effectiveness.

The BrandSPACE™[1] research tool (shown in Figure 9.1) measures this and:

- Helps find out whether or not the brand strategy is working – by tracking where a brand is in consumers' minds.
- Evaluates the level of emotional connection a brand has with the target audience.
- Provides insights to help sharpen brand positioning under circumstances of intense competition.
- Provides guideline to fine-tune brand image to stay competitive and achieve brand objectives.
- Tracks the effectiveness of brand expression and communication.
- Monitors share of heart and share of mind in addition to market share.

One of the interesting outputs of this brand management tool is the Passion Scorecard™, an easy-to-digest output that identifies key areas to

---

[1] Developed by Temporal Brand Consulting on license to Intage (Thailand) Co., Ltd. http://www.intage-thailand.com/proprietary01.php

Figure 9.1 The BrandSPACE™ Hearts and Minds Model.

focus on in order to strengthen the brand-customer relationship such as brand expression and communication, competitive advantage, customer's satisfaction or brand values/personality.

There are many ways of researching brand equity that look at rational and emotional impact of brand, but increasingly both public and private sector brands have become interested in assessing not just brand equity, but also the financial value of brands and the place they occupy in brand value rankings or indices. One such methodology that has been applied to private and public sector brands is illustrated below with respect to nations.

Measuring brand value

Brand valuation has come into play over the last two decades as a technique for justifying, and measuring returns on brand investment.

Brand management has now become the management of profitable strategic assets (brands) that can often be worth multiples of the net assets of the organization, institution or nation, and so the performance of brand managers is now becoming more closely evaluated on this basis.

There are many ranking tables for brand valuation that cover both public and private sectors, but among the most interesting for the public sector are those tables that appear annually for the brand value of nations. For purposes of illustration I shall use that created by Brand Finance plc, the world's leading independent valuation company (see Table 9.1). The methodology shown is that also used for valuing commercial brands.

Brand Finance's Nation Brand 100 measures the strength and value of the nation brands of leading countries using a method based on the royalty relief mechanism that Brand Finance uses to value the world's largest companies. The study provides each nation brand with a measure of its brand strength and a valuation of its brand value.[2]

The methodology described below is important in the sense that it can be used to measure the value of any public sector brand, and at the end of the day what is really important is not just the equity of the brand which is measured, but the value as well. Tracking the brand value annually via a scorecard mechanism reveals how various brand activities and policies impact in an economic way, in other words what actually drives the value of a brand. For nations, industries, non-profits and for profit public sector brands this gives an indication of what strategies work or don't, and can influence investors and analysts.

---

[2] www.brandfinance.com

Explanation of the Methodology

Nation Brands are quantified by total value using a 'royalty relief' method that quantifies the royalty that would be payable for a brand's use if it were controlled by a third party. The royalty rate is precisely calculated based on different sectors of the economy, and then applied to projected GDP over the next five years. A discount rate is then applied to this total to account for the time value of money and associated risk. This result quantifies the value that the brand brings to the economy.

The valuation of each nation brand is broken down into two distinct values (as shown below):

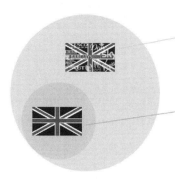

Step 1: Nation Brand + UK Product & Corporate Brands (Total GDP)
Includes all British Branded IP including product and corporate brands contributing to the UK GDP.

Step 2: Nation Brand only ('British' word mark and trademark iconography)
Includes the portion of UK GDP that is influenced by the nation brand. i.e., estimating how important the 'UK brand' is in driving business across the UK's primary, secondary and tertiary sectors.

Step 1a – Determine forecast GDP

- The first step in the valuation involves estimating future sales of all brands in each nation over a 5 year explicit forecast period.
- Gross domestic product (GDP) is used as a proxy for total revenues
- Forecast GDP is derived by reference to historic GDP trends and growth estimates from public and private organisations.
- GDP is segmented by economic segments (Primary, Secondary, and Tertiary) in order to take into consideration the role of product brands and the nation brand in each sector.

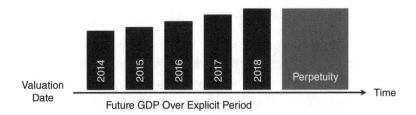

Valuation Date

Future GDP Over Explicit Period

Time

Economic Sectors		
Primary sectors including:	**Secondary** sectors including:	**Tertiary** sectors including:
Farming	Mining	Government activities
Fishing	Manufacturing	Communications
Forestry	Energy Production	Transportation
	Construction	Finance
		All other private economic activities that do not produce material goods

Step 1b – establish royalty rate range

- An analysis of publicly available license agreements is conducted in industries within primary, secondary and tertiary sectors using ktMINE[3]. The results are as follows:

Royalty Range based on sales			
	Primary	**Secondary**	**Tertiary**
Upper Quartile	8.0%	13.0%	19.0%
Lower Quartile	4.5%	3.8%	4.3%
Sample	78	2,753	2,081

---

[3] *ktMINE is one of the leading databases globally of commercial royalty agreements which contains details of over 30,000 intellectual property agreements*

- As you move from less sophisticated products in the primary sector towards more advanced services in the tertiary sector, the royalty rate increases in licensing agreements.
- This is because intellectual property tends to be more valuable in the more technically demanding, value added, products/services.
- The royalty rate ranges have been adjusted to take in to account outliers and the presence of other intellectual property that might be included in a license agreement such as patents, technical know-how, etc. The final result is what we believe to be a reasonable royalty rate range for the use of a trademark in each of the sectors:

Royalty Range					
Primary		**Secondary**		**Tertiary**	
	1.0%		1.0%		1.0%
Min	2.0%		2.0%		2.0%
	3.0%		3.0%		3.0%
	4.0%	**Min**	4.0%		4.0%
	5.0%		5.0%		5.0%
Max	6.0%		6.0%	**Min**	6.0%
	7.0%		7.0%		7.0%
	8.0%	**Max**	8.0%		8.0%
	9.0%		9.0%		9.0%
	10.0%		10.0%	**Max**	10.0%

Step 2a – establish royalty rate range for Nation Brand influence

- Royalty ranges are then adjusted to take into consideration the Nation Brand influence on each of the economic sectors.
- This analysis allows us to isolate nation brand portion in each sector.
- In our opinion, industries in the primary and secondary sector are highly influenced by the nation brand (e.g. Sri Lankan tea, German cars). In comparison, the nation brand may not be a significant driver of demand for tertiary sectors such as financial services. Therefore primary has a level of influence at 25 per cent, and tertiary at 15 per cent.

- Tertiary sector industry will typically command a higher royalty as it represents more "highly branded" industry, compared to the "less branded" commoditised primary sector.

Royalty Range							
Primary		Nation	**Secondary**		Nation	**Tertiary**	Nation
% Influence allocation		25%			20%		15%
Min	**2.0%**	0.5%					
			Min	**4.0%**	0.8%		
Max	**6.0%**	1.5%				**Min**	**6.0%**	0.9%
			Max	**8.0%**	1.6%		
						Max	**10.0%**	1.5%

Step 2b – assess the UK nation brand strength

- The Brand Strength Index ('BSI'), captures 195 measures across Investment, Goods and Services, People and Skills and Tourism (The Brand Finance Nation Brand Impact Framework) for the nation brand relative to competitor nation brands.
- These measures are used in a balanced scorecard framework to benchmark each nation against each other in determining an indexed score out of 100.
- Brand strength therefore measures both quality and size:
  - Quality – the equity the brand commands with users of the brand;
  - Size – the physical presence of the brand in the global market.
- The BSI is applied to the respective royalty range for each economic sector in order to determine the applicable royalty rate for primary, secondary and tertiary GDP segments.

- The BSI score for each particular nation is then applied to the necessary royalty rate range to determine an appropriate royalty rate.
- **For example:** The UK gets a brand strength score (BSI) of 74, which is applied to the royalty range identified for each sector to determine the applicable royalty rate for the Nation brand.

Royalty Range					
Primary % Influence allocation	Nation 25%	**Secondary**	Nation 20%	**Tertiary**	Nation 15%
Min 2.0%	0.5%	Min 4.0%	0.8%	Min 6.0%	0.9%
United Kingdom 4.9%	1.2%	United Kingdom 6.9%	1.4%	United Kingdom 8.9%	1.3%
Max 6.0%	1.5%	Max 8.0%	1.8%	Max 10.0%	1.5%

(74)

Step 3 – weighted average cost of capital ('WACC') or discount rate

- In order to account for the risk across each national economy a discount rate is calculated.
- The discount rate represents the average cost of a brand's sources of finance and the minimum return required on the brand asset.
- The discount rate is used to calculate the present value of future brand earnings (accounting for the time value of money and the associated risk).

$$\text{WACC} = (K_E \times (1 - P_D)) + (K_D \times P_D)$$

where

$$K_E = R_F + (R_E \times \beta_B)$$

K_E = Cost of Equity
P_D = Proportion of Debt
R_F = Risk Free Rate
R_E = Equity Risk Premium
β_B = Brand Beta

and

$$K_D = (R_F + B_R) \times (1 - \text{Tax})$$

K_D = Cost of Debt
P_D = Proportion of Debt
R_F = Risk Free Rate
β_R = Brand Risk Premium

Step 4 – long-term growth rate

- The nation brand valuation is based on 5 year forecasts. In addition, an annuity is calculated on the final year's brand contribution to account for the value of the nation brand into perpetuity.
- The long term growth rate taken from the long term economic growth forecasts, sourced from OECD.

Step 5 – brand valuation

- The calculated royalty rates for primary, secondary and tertiary GDP are multiplied to the appropriate segmented GDP to derive a "total brand contribution," which is taxed at the local corporate tax rate.
- The brand contribution after tax is discounted back to a "net present value" using the discount rate.
- Added to the discounted value into perpetuity you derive the "nation brand value."
- This valuation calculation is completed for all segments which are totalled together for the total brand value.

Illustration of one segment's brand valuation schedule:

All figures in US$ billions	2013	2014	2015	2016	2017	2018	Perpetuity
GDP (Tertiary)	2,015	2,076	2,130	2,187	2,249	2,310	
Royalty Rate applicable to PRIMARY('British' word mark and trademark iconography)		1.3%	1.3%	1.3%	1.3%	1.3%	
Total brand contribution		28	29	29	30	31	
Tax rate		21%	21%	21%	21%	21%	
Brand contribution after tax		22	23	23	24	25	
Discount rate (10%)		1.10	1.20	1.32	1.45	1.59	
Present value		20	19	18	16	15	
Net present value							88
Perpetuity							268
Brand value							356

Benefits summary of nation branding to governments and steps for implementation

At a high level, the brand valuation framework for nation brands provides a scorecard approach for understanding, tracking and diagnosing a nation brand. More detailed analysis is needed to understand a nation in its various segments in order to help drive GDP. Gaining an understanding of a nation's economy at a macro and micro level, and understanding how it performs against its peers in each component allows for superior nation brand strategic agility and focus.

A "macro level" understanding of the nation brand

This is a high level focus on the nation as a whole. It involves engagement with key nation brand stakeholders, such as government ministers, top civil servants, and major business leaders from a range of sectors, to come together for high level discussions, brain storming, debate and visioning in order to understand the tools available to a nation for promoting greater GDP creation.

Steps include:

- Exploring an inspiring vision for the nation brand.
- Reputation, perception vs. reality of the nation brand.
- Current issues with maximising the nation brand.
- The nation's strengths weakness, opportunities and threats (SWOT) within the Nation Brand Impact™ segments – Investment, Tourism, Product and Talent.
- A decomposition, analysis and thorough understanding of the nation's GDP to identify contributions by sector.
- Examining perceptions of the nation brand and which brand narratives are and are not being successfully communicated.
- An evaluation of where the nation stands in terms of its stage of development e.g. emerging, innovation driven.

Table 9.1 The Top 100 Nation Brands 2014

Rank 2014	Rank 2013	Nation Brand	Economy Type	Region	BRAND VALUE 2014 (Represents the Nation Brand + UK Product & Corporate Brands (Total GDP))	BRAND VALUE 2014 (Represents the Nation Brand only ('Nation' word mark and trademark iconography))	BRAND VALUE 2013 (Represents the Nation Brand + UK Product & Corporate Brands (Total GDP))	BRAND VALUE 2013 (Represents the Nation Brand only ('Nation' word mark and trademark iconography))	Brand Strength Rating 2014	Brand Strength Rating 2013
1	1	United States	Advanced Economy	North America	19,261	3,089	17,990	2,848	AA+	AA
2	2	China	Emerging and developing Asia	Asia	6,352	1,127	6,109	1,081	AA–	AA–
3	3	Germany	Advanced Economy	Europe	4,357	709	4,002	649	AA+	AA
4	4	United Kingdom	Advanced Economy	Europe	2,833	449	2,354	375	AA	AA
5	5	Japan	Advanced Economy	Asia	2,458	401	2,263	365	AA–	AA–
6	7	Canada	Advanced Economy	North America	2,212	366	1,863	303	AA–	AA
7	6	France	Advanced Economy	Europe	2,076	329	1,938	308	AA–	AA–
8	9	India	Emerging and developing Asia	Asia	1,621	275	1,366	235	A+	A+
9	10	Australia	Advanced Economy	Pacific	1,555	258	1,257	206	AA	AA
10	8	Brazil	Latin America and Caribbean	South America	1,403	232	1,478	242	A	A+
11	12	Italy	Advanced Economy	Europe	1,289	208	1,043	168	A+	A
12	11	Russian Federation	Commonwealth of independent states	Europe	1,246	209	1,257	211	A–	A–
13	14	Switzerland	Advanced Economy	Europe	1,151	186	965	157	AA+	AA+
14	15	Mexico	Latin America and Caribbean	Central America	1,027	170	807	134	A	A
15	13	Netherlands	Advanced Economy	Europe	1,026	165	997	161	AA	AA
16	16	Korea, Rep.	Advanced Economy	Asia	997	168	775	131	AA–	AA–
17	17	Sweden	Advanced Economy	Europe	802	129	752	122	AA	AA
18	18	Spain	Advanced Economy	Europe	801	130	725	118	A+	A+
19	19	Turkey	Emerging and developing Europe	Europe	751	126	688	115	A+	A+
20	20	Poland	Emerging and developing Europe	Europe	602	101	497	85	A	A

21	21	Austria	Advanced Economy	Europe	471	77	439	72	AA-	AA
22	22	Saudi Arabia	Middle East, Nth Africa & Pakistan	Middle East	463	84	420	76	A	A
23	24	Singapore	Advanced Economy	Asia	460	76	404	65	AA+	AA+
24	23	Belgium	Advanced Economy	Europe	452	72	420	67	AA-	AA-
25	27	Taiwan, China	Advanced Economy	Asia	414	69	339	57	AA-	AA
26	26	Thailand	Emerging and developing Asia	Asia	409	72	359	64	AA-	AA-
27	29	Norway	Advanced Economy	Europe	396	67	330	56	AA-	AA-
28	28	Indonesia	Emerging and developing Asia	Asia	395	70	339	61	A+	A+
29	25	Denmark	Advanced Economy	Europe	394	63	369	59	AA-	AA-
30	30	Malaysia	Emerging and developing Asia	Asia	386	67	304	53	AA	AA
31	31	Finland	Advanced Economy	Europe	307	51	287	47	AA-	AA-
32	34	United Arab Emirates	Middle East, Nth Africa & Pakistan	Middle East	292	52	249	44	AA-	AA-
33	33	Argentina	Latin America and Caribbean	South America	265	45	255	43	A-	A-
34	36	Philippines	Emerging and developing Asia	Asia	260	45	193	33	A	A
35	32	South Africa	Sub-Saharan Africa	Africa	256	42	270	44	A+	A+
36	39	Qatar	Middle East, Nth Africa & Pakistan	Middle East	256	48	184	34	A+	AA-
37	35	Chile	Latin America and Caribbean	South America	250	43	202	34	A+	A+
38	38	Ireland	Advanced Economy	Europe	250	40	185	30	AA-	AA-
39	37	Hong Kong SAR	Advanced Economy	Asia	226	35	193	29	AA-	AA
40	41	New Zealand	Advanced Economy	Pacific	191	31	152	25	AA-	AA
41	40	Czech Republic	Advanced Economy	Europe	180	31	154	26	A	A+
42	44	Vietnam	Emerging and developing Asia	Asia	172	31	133	24	A	A
43	42	Peru	Latin America and Caribbean	South America	171	29	146	25	A	A
44	48	Kazakhstan	Commonwealth of independent states	Asia	164	28	120	20	A-	A-

(continued)

235

Table 9.1 *(continued)*

Rank 2014	Rank 2013	Nation Brand	Economy Type	Region	BRAND VALUE 2014 (Represents the Nation Brand + UK Product & Corporate Brands (Total GDP))	BRAND VALUE 2014 (Represents the Nation Brand only ('Nation' word mark and trademark iconography))	BRAND VALUE 2013 (Represents the Nation Brand + UK Product & Corporate Brands (Total GDP))	BRAND VALUE 2013 (Represents the Nation Brand only ('Nation' word mark and trademark iconography))	Brand Strength Rating 2014	Brand Strength Rating 2013
45	47	Colombia	Latin America and Caribbean	South America	159	27	120	20	A–	A–
46	43	Israel	Advanced Economy	Middle East	151	24	138	23	A	A–
47	49	Nigeria	Sub-Saharan Africa	Africa	132	25	111	21	BBB	BBB
48	46	Romania	Emerging and developing Europe	Europe	127	22	121	20	A–	A–
49	52	Bangladesh	Emerging and developing Asia	Asia	115	20	83	14	BBB	A–
50	51	Portugal	Advanced Economy	Europe	114	18	91	15	A+	A+
51	50	Kuwait	Middle East, Nth Africa & Pakistan	Middle East	100	18	106	18	BBB	A–
52	45	Ukraine	Commonwealth of independent states	Europe	83	14	126	21	A–	A–
53	53	Hungary	Emerging and developing Europe	Europe	82	14	75	12	A–	A
54	54	Egypt	Middle East, Nth Africa & Pakistan	Africa	75	13	70	12	BBB	BBB
55	56	Pakistan	Middle East, Nth Africa & Pakistan	Asia	72	13	64	11	A–	A–
56	58	Algeria	Middle East, Nth Africa &. Pakistan	Africa	66	12	52	10	BB	BB
57	57	Slovak Republic	Advanced Economy	Europe	65	11	57	9	A–	A–
58	65	Sri Lanka	Emerging and developing Asia	Asia	61	10	45	8	A+	A+
59	61	Greece	Advanced Economy	Europe	61	10	48	8	A–	BBB
60	62	Slovenia	Advanced Economy	Europe	56	9	47	8	A–	A
61	59	Luxembourg	Advanced Economy	Europe	56	9	52	8	A+	AA–

62	60	Omar	Middle East, Nth Africa & Pakistani	Middle East	53	10	49	9	A-	A
63	63	Dominican Republic	Latin America and Caribbean	Central America	53	9	45	8	A-	A-
64	67	Morocco	Middle East, Nth Africa & Pakistan	Africa	48	8	40	7	A	A-
65	64	Bulgaria	Emerging and developing Europe	Europe	45	7	45	8	BBB	A-
66	69	Ecuador	Latin America and Caribbean	South America	44	8	36	6	BBB	BBB
67	70	Lithuania	Emerging and developing Europe	Europe	44	7	35	6	A-	A
68	68	Costa Rica	Latin America and Caribbean	Central America	43	7	38	6	A	A
69	74	Panama	Latin America and Caribbean	Central America	40	6	32	5	A-	A-
70	71	Azerbaijan	Commonwealth of independent states	Asia	39	7	34	6	A	A-
71	72	Jordan	Middle East, Nth Africa & Pakistan	Middle East	38	6	33	5	A-	A
72	73	Guatemala	Latin America and Caribbean	Central America	37	6	33	6	A-	A-
73	66	Croatia	Emerging and developing Europe	Europe	36	6	40	7	A	A
74	75	Serbia	Emerging and developing Europe	Europe	34	6	31	5	BBB	BBB
75	78	Latvia	Advanced Economy	Europe	33	5	27	4	A-	A-
76	76	Uruguay	Latin America and Caribbean	South America	33	5	30	5	A-	A-
77	79	Bahrain	Middle East, Nth Africa & Pakistan	Middle East	28	5	25	4	A	A
78	77	Lebanon	Middle East, Nth Africa & Pakistan	Middle East	22	3	28	5	BBB	A-
79	81	Kenya	Sub-Saharan Africa	Africa	22	4	19	3	A-	A
80	82	Paraguay	Latin America and Caribbean	South America	21	4	17	3	BBB	BBB
81	80	Ghana	Sub-Saharan Africa	Africa	21	4	20	3	BBB	BBB
82	85	Estonia	Advanced Economy	Europe	19	3	15	2	A+	A+
83	86	Ethiopia	Sub-Saharan Africa	Africa	18	3	14	3	BBB	BBB

(continued)

Table 9.1 (continued)

Rank 2014	Rank 2013	Nation Brand	Economy Type	Region	BRAND VALUE 2014 (Represents the Nation Brand + UK Product & Corporate Brands (Total GDP))	BRAND VALUE 2014 (Represents the Nation Brand only ('Nation' word mark and trademark iconography))	BRAND VALUE 2013 (Represents the Nation Brand + UK Product & Corporate Brands (Total GDP))	BRAND VALUE 2013 (Represents the Nation Brand only ('Nation' word mark and trademark iconography))	Brand Strength Rating 2014	Brand Strength Rating 2013
84	83	Bolivia	Latin America and Caribbean	South America	17	3	16	3	BBB	A–
85	88	Tanzania	Sub-Saharan Africa	Africa	16	3	13	2	BBB	BBB
86	84	El Salvador	Latin America and Caribbean	Central America	16	3	15	2	A–	A–
87	87	Cyprus	Advanced Economy	Europe	15	2	14	2	A	A
88	91	Cambodia	Emerging and developing Asia	Asia	15	3	12	2	A	A
89	90	Bosnia and Herzegovina	Emerging and developing Europe	Europe	15	2	12	2	BBB	BBB
90	89	Honduras	Latin America and Caribbean	Central America	14	2	13	2	A–	A–
91	92	Georgia	Commonwealth of independent states	Asia	13	2	12	2	BBB	BBB
92	94	Uganda	Sub-Saharan, Africa	Africa	12	2	10	2	BBB	A–
93	93	Iceland	Advanced Economy	Europe	11	2	11	2	A+	A+
94	95	Nepal	Emerging and developing Asia	Asia	11	2	9	2	BBB	BBB
95	98	Brunei Darussalam	Emerging and developing Asia	Asia	10	2	9	2	A	A
96	96	Cameroon	Sub-Saharan Africa	Africa	10	2	9	2	BB	BBB
97	97	Botswana	Sub-Saharan Africa	Africa	10	2	9	2	A–	A–
98	99	Zambia	Sub-Saharan Africa	Africa	10	2	8	1	BBB	BBB
99	100	Albania	Emerging and developing Europe	Europe	9	1	8	1	A–	BBB
100		Jamaica	Latin America and Caribbean	Central America	8	1	–	–	A	A–

A granular "micro Level' understanding of the nation brand

A granular level analysis of sectors within the nation's economy clarifies what drives national GDP and enables a government to set clear priorities of development for sector and sub-sectors of strategic importance. This includes analysis and examination of the core competencies of each sector to provide insight on potential areas for developing new competitive and comparative advantages regionally and globally, as well as enhancing current ones. This leads to a clear design of a sector-wide brand plan covering the planned investment, implementation, brand and sub-brand architecture, and interaction with the nation brand.

Steps include:

- Conducting a detailed analysis of the sector strengths, weaknesses, opportunities, threats regionally and globally.
- Researching and understanding the core competencies of the sector and sub-sectors.
- Segmenting and prioritising audiences and motivations for each segment.
- Gaining insight into audience aspirations and perceptions in each segment.
- Using a sector level drill-down of the "nation attractiveness" tool to collate research to provide sector insights for analysis into issues and ways to maximise the sectors brands.

Implementation and monitoring

The final stage of the nation brand process is the implementation of nation- and sector-level plans for nation brand development that are agreed in concert with stakeholders through a multi-step development strategy. The creation of a monitoring framework allows for future performance tracking of a nation brand by segment against all of the nation brand's attributes.

Summary

The nation brand methodology mentioned above is one of a few, however, it is probably the most rigorous and reliable. The message is that even at national brand level, there is a need to track the success of public sector brands and that this can be done. As in the private sector, tracking is best done on the basis of increases or decreases in value and where that value comes from, in addition to carrying out brand audits that look at image equity and perceptions as mentioned earlier in this chapter. A comprehensive view is required and brand tracking should be done on a regular annual basis as customer needs and competitor activity change.

Summary of Part Two

There are several important points that arise from the discussions in Chapters 6 to 9 of this section.

- A well-constructed brand strategy is unlikely to be successful without correct implementation.
- Implementation of brand strategy includes strong brand management, relevant communications, internal engagement, and measurement of success.
- A brand communications strategy defining the key messages to transmit to all target audiences is essential to keep messaging consistent while allowing for the tailoring of messages to different audiences in order to keep them relevant. The ability to keep the central message of the brand consistent while keeping the creative execution fresh is a delicate process that has to be carefully managed.
- The nature of brand communications is changing very quickly with the advent of new technologies and media. The public sector must use these platforms, especially social media and mobile, to best effect in both dealing with crises and threats to brand image, and in building brand equity and value. This involves learning how to talk to audiences in real time and embracing brand democracy.
- Brand engagement, sometimes referred to as brand alignment or internal branding, is critical if the promise of a brand is to be delivered. Everyone in a public sector organization has to know what the brand stands for, what it means for their work, and how they can contribute. Continuous training is vital for enhancement of the customer experience as the external brand image of an organization will never be better than its internal image.
- Brand management is a holistic and on-going process that seeks to manage all that a brand does and says. In particular, it is concerned with making sure that the desired identity of the brand is matched by its perceived image. While not all factors that influence brand image are under the control of those responsible for brand management, it is

important that all issues and activities are monitored and controlled as well as possible.

- The holistic management of a brand is best achieved through a structure designed for specifically that purpose. Such a structure should involve strategic direction from the top of the organization and ideas and implementation at all levels below. It is a two-way process, and inclusiveness is vitally important.
- Finally, all brand activities should be monitored and measured for success. This can be carried out in many ways and may involve the measurement of factors that influence brand equity. In addition, it is best to measure the value of the brand and use this as an annual indicator of brand strength. In other words, if you can't measure it don't do it!

Chapter 10

The Future of Public Sector Branding

A s with the private sector, the public sector is faced with intense competition for investment, talent, business and trade, tourism, favourable government policies, or membership that shares a similar cause or set of beliefs.

The public sector is using the same techniques of branding as those used by private sector companies, and branding has been recognized as a strategic activity that must be backed up by strong brand management.

National brands and emerging markets

There is no doubt at all that nations are going to become even more involved in branding activities in order to achieve strategic national objectives. There will always be the need for increasing exports and developing international trade, the promotion of tourism and national culture, the attraction of foreign direct investment, and the acquisition of talent. These four main objectives are not only relevant to developed economies but also for developing countries trying to achieve developed nation status. The push on branding from developing countries is indicated in the BrandFinance® Nation Brands 2013 report, where we see some examples of them in the "top movers" lists for the four categories of Tourism (Sri Lanka and Estonia), Goods and Services (Pakistan and Indonesia),

Investment (Philippines and Lithuania), and People and Skills (Bangladesh and Cambodia).

A second reason why branding in the public sector will become more prominent is because of the need to overcome damaged national images caused by internal strife. The unfortunate hostilities and civil wars that have been observed in recent years, particularly in the Middle East, will eventually lead new and stable governments to pursue policies, diplomacy and conventional branding techniques in order to regain favourable relationships, reputation, and images that will improve their economic and social circumstances. Some countries such as Thailand have to do this every few years as the political roller coaster continues to produce a degree of instability.

Geopolitical changes such as interactions and "movement" of sections of countries to others, as witnessed recently between Russia and the Ukraine, will also eventually lead to the need for re-positioning. Economic sanctions and other political actions will eventually be replaced by the need to improve economically and establish better brand images. Iran is moving through this process at present. Indeed, changes of government often bring changes in policies that have pronounced effects on country brand images, offering both challenges and opportunities.

While strong public sector brands survive most disruptions as they do in the private sector, weaker brands will find it harder. This is particularly true of developed (stronger brands) versus developing (weaker brands) nations and markets. However, no country can afford to neglect its brand or fail to build and manage it. As David Haigh, CEO of Brand Finance plc says, "A strong brand has become a defining feature of success in the current economic climate. Worldwide hyper-competition for business, combined with an increasingly cluttered media environment, means that the clear message carried by a properly-managed brand can provide the crucial leverage needed to thrive. The financial uplift provided to a product or corporation from a strong brand is well known, and companies invest heavily in protecting their brands. Nations can adopt similar techniques to capitalize on the economic growth that comes with proper positioning of a nation brand. All nations should be working actively to realize this potential."[1]

Strategic industries, destinations and cities

Nations will also continue to try and elevate the images of their strategic industries; those industries considered essential for growth and development. In some cases they will need to regain some lost ground, such as Taiwan in information technology. In other circumstances they will be looking to move from an image of a manufacturing and commodities-based economy to a service economy, a task currently faced by emerging economies such as Malaysia, and one that China will face in the not-too-distant future. Some will drive further down the brand path to develop more global awareness and success, such as Dubai (United Arab Emirates) in tourism. Other more developed nations will have to hang on to their existing brand equity and value in their chosen industries, such as Singapore in infocomms technology and Britain in the automotive industry.

Tourism will certainly remain a global focus, as this is a relatively easy, although highly competitive, industry to engage in branding activities. And more cities and place destinations within countries will become involved in the search for visitors and investors.

Building the Nation Brand Effect

Much of the future of branding activity at both national and corporate levels will come from emerging markets, especially in Asia, but also the fast-developing countries of Europe. The Nation Brand Effect (NBE) in these countries needs a lot of attention so that corporations can grow, become

---

[1] Brand Finance Nation Brands, The annual report on nation brands, December 2013.

successful, and act as brand ambassadors. Given that in many of these markets, companies are either government-linked or influenced in their actions by government policies (good or bad), emerging-market governments have to focus on developing, not just the national brand, but their corporate brands as well, as South Korea has done in the past to a substantial effect.

According to Kumar and Steenkamp[2] there are several hurdles that need to be overcome in this process, which include:

- Improving transparency, especially in ownership structures and governance standards.
- Enhancing profitability and integrity of financial statements, for example, putting greater emphasis in statements on market share (which can make a situation look better), instead of profitability (where disclosure of low margins may make things look worse).
- Moving from imitation to innovation, when product replication may be acceptable to the domestic market but not to international markets where differentiation is a key driver of success.
- Acceptance of management diversity and a global mind set. When building brands internationally, there is a need to involve talent (especially at senior levels) from the target markets and integrate them into the organizational culture. This not only applies to organizations from emerging countries but also to those from developed countries wanting to move into emerging markets.

Indeed, in order to rise up the competitiveness rankings, and to be able to join multinational branded "clubs" such as the European Community, all of these items and more need to be given attention, and branding activities by governments should be accorded a high priority on the policy-making agenda. I would add one more aspect of public sector that nations are now beginning to look at in both the developed and developing world,

---

[2] Kumar, N. and Steenkamp, J-B.E.M., *Brand Breakout: How Emerging Market Brands Will Go Global*, Palgrave Macmillan, 2013.

and that is the transformation and branding of the public service (sometimes called the civil service).

Branding the public service

The public service is at the interface of practically everything a nation
does. Its ministries, departments and statutory boards all have multiple
touchpoints with citizens, the private sector, government-linked corporations and non-profit organizations as well as tourists, investors, talent and
other target audiences outside the country. The efficiency and effectiveness of the public service thus determines to a great extent the national
brand image and its global competitiveness rankings. Indeed the public
service is becoming a defining part of a nation's competitive edge.

Several countries are now engaged in transformational processes to
enhance the efficiency, effectiveness and image of their public service. The
UK in the West is one country that is undergoing transformation in its civil
service, and Malaysia in the East is another. But while many countries are
focusing on efficiency and effectiveness perhaps the most interesting example from a branding perspective is that of the Canadian public service.

CASE STUDY: Branding the public service of Canada

Introduction
In 2007 the Canada Public Service Agency unveiled a major plan to
brand the public service of Canada.[3] Although many government
organizations such as the Canada Post Corporation and Canadian

(continued)

---

[3] Delivered to a conference on "The Shifting Sands of Public Sector Delivery" at Dalhousie
University, November 2007 by Ms Denise Amyot. www.cappa.ca/index/php/en/

Museum of Civilization had been the subject of branding activities, the importance of branding the public service was seen to be an important next step. In short, the reasons for doing so were listed as follows:

- To support government's plan for a stronger Canada.
- To support one of the key objectives of the government to strengthen and promote Canada's foundational values of freedom, democracy, human rights and the rule of law.
- To build employees' trust and pride, and encourage them to act as ambassadors for their organization, its values, products and services.
- To attract and recruit qualified new employees.
- To reflect government's efforts in ensuring that the public service meets the evolving needs of Canadians and the Canadian society with excellence in policy development and advice, and professional service delivery.

The stimulus for this brand exercise had come from a number of market research studies about the public service including a set of findings from the Qualitative Research with the Canadian Public and Public Servants on Trust, Accountability and the Management Agenda (The Strategic Counsel, October 2005). The findings from this research study revealed three important issues, namely:

- There continues to be a credibility gap with the public and public servants.
- Canadians want to hear what it has done and how it matters to them.
- Most employees lack the "big picture" of the government and have difficulty explaining how what they do matters in Canadians' lives, unless they work directly with the public.

One further piece of research stated that, "Only 8% of male youth and 3% of female respondents think that the federal government is the most interesting work place to pursue a career." (Reconnecting with Youth, 2006, Ipsos-Reid).

The four main target audiences for the overall public service (PS) master brand were thus potential employees, current employees, parliamentarians and Canadians in general. Other research had backed up these findings, and a great deal of analysis took place regarding what perceptions of the public service were held by these main target audiences, what was important to them, what the perception gaps were, and what areas the PS brand could work on to close these gaps. Other consultations took place with those PS departments and agencies that had relevant experience, especially those that had been involved in branding activities.

Brand architecture
Given that the target audiences were different in terms of expectations and needs, and that some departments had already carried out branding activities for various purposes, it was clear that any PS brand development would need to be flexible in order to accommodate these sub-brands and allow for a degree of customization to suit their particular needs. An umbrella brand approach was therefore necessary that would provide not only consistency in terms of a commonly-held and communicated vision, mission and values, but also allow different departments and other organizations within the public service (sub-brands) to have some autonomy in terms of their own marketing and key messages for communication. This balancing act is never easy for any organization, especially a large one such as a public service, and provides many challenges for organizational brand managers.

(continued)

The public service brand management structure
At a very early stage in the whole process a structure was put into place to ensure proper development and management of the PS brand. This structure included a Brand Working Committee consisting of officials from various agencies and departments, a Steering Committee of Assistant Deputy Ministers and senior officials from across the public, and an Expert Advisory Group (non-governmental) to be used as a sounding board. It is important to note that union officials were also included at committee level to get buy-in and support and gain full representation. In other words, all key stakeholders were engaged in some form or other in order to gather information, achieve buy-in and garner full support for the brand promise and implementation activities.

It was decided that an integrated and strategic approach to branding was necessary not just from a client viewpoint but also for internal employee communication and to approach potential new recruits.

Brand development
Following the internal and external research phases, the PS brand was carefully crafted including a brand vision, mission, values, promise and character (the identity) and positioning. All were tested via consultation with the committees and departments before the implementation framework was put in place, and the result was a solid, well-tested brand strategy. While the overall mission was to "serve the public and the public interest," the brand vision encompassed the main strategic thrust and goals of the PS brand, "The public service of Canada is a world-class institution attracting, motivating and engaging highly-skilled people to serve the public and the public interest."[4]

---

[4] *Ibid.*

The PS brand values were placed into four categories:

• Democratic: Helping ministers, under law, to serve the public interest.
• Professional: serving with competence, excellence, efficiency, objectivity and impartiality.
• Ethical: Acting at all times in such a way as to uphold public trust.
• People: Demonstrating respect, fairness and courtesy in their dealings with both citizens and fellow public servants.

Brand implementation

Subsequently to the development of the PS brand, a comprehensive action plan was created that had activities running every month while on-going development and tracking were evaluated with various stakeholders. Implementing the brand promise consisted of developing visual identity, messaging and actions. The team developed both a communications strategy, and engagement and outreach strategy, and much of the early activities were communications-oriented and tailored to the target audiences. The expected benefits of the PS brand development and its sustained activities were the attraction of more highly-skilled talent, retention and motivation of current employees and a better image of the public service with Canadian citizens.

(A fifth and more minor international community target audience was also considered. Although little is written about this audience, one could assume that improvements to the PS image inside Canada would inevitably bring similar improvements outside Canada for those who interacted with the PS).

Some of the challenges found in developing and implementing the PS brand included the task of being relevant to all target audiences and stakeholders in such a diverse organization. Positioning and messaging can be particularly challenging as among the main target audiences there are many sub-segments. For example, among prospective employees there are graduates, young professionals, mid-career recruits and senior executives.

(continued)

Summary

This case study is only a brief summary of the considerable detail contained in the documents that are publically available, and in my opinion, it is worth reading about in full as there is much to learn from the Canadian public service branding exercise. I will close this case by quoting from the Canadian documents what a brand is, which is symptomatic of those leaders who really understand branding and should be noted by all public sector branding leaders and teams.

"A brand is a promise made to clients to deliver clearly stated benefits that are valued and that set it apart from its competitors – it is much more than a logo, a tagline or a slogan."

The public service, as mentioned above, is the bridge between government and both domestic and international markets and interacts with the private sector extensively. In addition to this inter-connectivity I believe that in the wider non-government area there will be more interaction and partnerships between commercial and public sector brands, especially non-profits, with more emphasis on helping communities. This will include corporate social responsibility and shared value initiatives, together with new forms of collaboration and I would like to discuss some of them now.

Corporate social responsibility and global partnerships

Globally, consumers are now demanding that private and public sector organizations and entities demonstrate a greater degree of ethics and consideration for communities in their strategies. In other words, more social responsibility.

Private sector companies vary in their commitment to corporate social responsibility, with some merely giving to charities and some going further and incorporating it into their code of ethics and brand DNA. The Body Shop is one obvious example of this, but a less well-known one is Innocent Drinks.

CASE STUDY: Innocent Drinks

Innocent Drinks, a UK-based company best known for their smoothies and quirky brand messaging is actively involved in several cause-related marketing initiatives. It says very clearly on its delightfully refreshing website that, "we want innocent to become a global, natural, ethical food and drinks company, always remaining commercially successful and socially aware." The brand values for innocent are:

- natural
- entrepreneurial
- responsible
- commercial
- generous

And the brand promise is "Tastes good. Does good."

Each year, innocent donates a percentage of the company profits to charity. The majority of this is channeled to the Innocent Foundation which aims to improve the lives of the rural community dependent on sustainable agriculture in countries where innocent's fruits are sourced from. In September 2007, innocent became the first company in the world to launch a bottle made from 100 per cent recycled plastic. Other sustainable characteristics in innocent's packaging include using the least possible amount of material per pack, using materials with a low-carbon footprint and using materials for which there is a widely available sustainable waste-management option.

The ingredients for innocent's drinks are also sourced in a responsible manner. Buying priority is given to farms that look after the interests of both the environment and the workers. For example, all of innocent's bananas are Rainforest Alliance certified and they also aim to be a resource-efficient business by paying close attention to their

(continued)

carbon and water footprints, actively seeking to lower both in their business activities.[5]

Although innocent sold a 20 per cent stake in its business to Coca-Cola in 2009, it says it will not change its ethical vision. Co-founder, Richard Reed said, "Every promise that innocent has made, about making only natural healthy products, pioneering the use of better, socially- and environmentally-aware ingredients, packaging and production techniques, donating money to charity and having a point of view on the world will remain. We'll just get to do them even more."[6]

The Innocent Foundation is involved in many partnerships. It provides funding so that non-profits can focus more on their work and less on fund-raising. They offer funding to charities all over the world for four types of projects (*www.innocentfoundation.org/what-we-fund*):

1. **Seed Funding** – helping partner charities get new projects underway.
2. **UK Food Poverty** – helping charities working on UK food poverty projects from early 2014.
3. **Breakthrough Development** – a new funding area in 2014 to take risks on new, untested ideas to find new models to help address hunger issues.
4. **Emergency Hunger Relief** – making donations in order to have a direct and immediate impact on those affected by major disasters.

Partnerships

Innocent has teamed up with partners from the non-profit world, including their Livewell campaign[7] with WWF, bringing the topics of health and sustainability together, about which it says, "We're proud

---

[5] www.innocentdrinks.co.uk/us/ethics/

[6] BBC News, "Coke buys into Innocent smoothies", 7 April 2009, news.bbc.co.uk/1/hi/7986901.stm

[7] www.innocentdrinks.co.uk/us/being-sustainable/nutrition

of our Livewell campaign. It was the first time we'd brought the topics of health and sustainability together, and it made a lot of sense to do so, as together they form the very bedrock of our business. And they're intricately connected.

"We wanted to find a way to talk about the fact that what and how you choose to eat can make a massive difference not only to your own health and wellbeing, but to that of the planet too.

"To illustrate this concept, we teamed up with the WWF UK and an independent expert, and spoke about 'sustainable nutrition' within the context of the WWF's Livewell principles."[8]

Many foundations take a similar donor-based economic approach, but some private sector businesses are now moving towards a shared-value approach, where they change their business models to help deliver more collective impact with the communities they are trying to help.

Social innovation, collective impact and creating shared value

One of the most promising trends in brand building today is the way in which the private and public sectors are coming together to establish radical ways of achieving major outcomes in a variety of social sectors. Social Innovation is a relatively new concept that connects business strategy with corporate social responsibility and philanthropy. It is clearly a trend that will continue to manifest itself, witnessed by the growing number of public and private sector partnerships, especially with private sector companies that have an ethical side to their purpose embedded in their brand DNA that want to achieve more collective impact. Although many still do so, companies are moving away from merely putting aside budgets for philanthropic purposes as they have done for many years under

---

[8] *Ibid.*

the heading of corporate social responsibility. Indeed, corporate social responsibility is evolving into more sustainable ways of providing for solutions to social problems, which can vary in scale and complexity.

John Kania and Mark Kramer, writing in the Stanford Social Innovation Review discuss Mars (manufacturer of chocolate brands including M&M's and Snickers) as an example of a company working with NGOs, local governments and direct competitors to improve the lives of impoverished cocoa farmers in Côte d'Ivoire, where a large portion of cocoa is sourced by Mars. They explain how a coordinated effort from multiple organizations is required in order to obtain more agricultural workers, finance new roads and reach farmers outside its supply chain.

However, the authors comment that while the evidence of the effectiveness of this approach is currently limited, more progress could be made if such companies were aligned around a more common agenda and that: "It doesn't happen often, not because it is impossible, but because it is so rarely attempted. Funders and nonprofits alike overlook the potential for collective impact because they are used to focusing on independent action as the primary vehicle for social change."[9]

Despite this concern, many more companies are moving in the direction of social innovation and collective impact, for example, Hewlett-Packard (HP).

HP has progressed from technology provisions to causes, and is exploring an approach that challenges health and education problems through technological solutions developed by its staff. The company has worked with mPedigree Network, an African social enterprise, to create a system in order to resolve the issue of counterfeit drugs which accounts for approximately 700 000 deaths worldwide each year. Through cloud computing

---

[9] Kania, John and Kramer, Mark, "Collective impact", *Stanford Social Innovation Review,* Vol 9: 1, Winter 2011, www.ssireview.org/articles/entry/collective_impact

and mobile technologies a solution was found: a secure code is printed on the packaging of the drugs, and consumers who consume medication from May & Baker Nigeria PLC and the KAMA Group of Ghana can text the code to the system, free of charge, to ensure that the drugs are genuine.

"Over the years, we have invested a huge amount of time and money in developing drugs which will protect the health of people around the world," said Dr Joseph Ikemefuna Odumodu, chief executive, May & Baker Nigeria, and president of the West African Pharmaceutical Manufacturers Association. "It's in both our and our customers' interest that they receive the full benefit of that investment. This system will safeguard both of us now and in the future."

HP is providing the hosting infrastructure for the service, as well as the security and integrity systems through its data centres in Frankfurt, Germany. mPedigree Network is providing the business process interfaces that allow pharmaceutical companies to code their products for the system and to monitor use of genuine and counterfeit drugs.

The service, which is endorsed by the West African Health Organization, is expected to be available for other medications and in more countries in future. All GSM-mobile network operators in Ghana and Nigeria are signatories to the scheme.

The founder of mPedigree Network, Bright Simons, explained that "counterfeit pharmaceuticals are a big problem for developing nations, particularly in Africa. It's absolutely imperative that people can trust the authenticity of the drugs they are consuming, and this system will give them an easy and effective way of doing so." This service is in use in Nigeria and Ghana (where over 40 per cent of anti-malarial drugs are counterfeit) and is being extended to other countries this year. What makes this system successful is the fact that the concept is easy, cheap and accessible as 75 per cent of people using anti-malarial drugs have access to mobile phones.

Gabriele Zedlmayer, Vice President, Office of Global Social Innovation, HP says: "Technology plays a critical role in solving many serious health problems around the world...While Nigeria and Ghana are the starting points for this programme, we are working to create a scalable infrastructure to be used by other regions where counterfeit medicine is a growing issue."[10]

Social entrepreneurship and creating shared value (CSV)

Social innovation can also be associated with social entrepreneurship, where someone recognizes a social problem and uses entrepreneurial skills to organize, create and manage a venture to achieve social change. Whereas a business entrepreneur typically measures performance in profit and return, a social entrepreneur focuses on creating social capital. Thus, the main aim of social entrepreneurship is to further social and environmental goals. However, whilst social entrepreneurs are most commonly associated with the voluntary and not-for-profit sectors, this need not necessarily be incompatible with making a profit. Social entrepreneurship practised with a world view or in an international context is sometimes called international social entrepreneurship. Social entrepreneurship initiatives often work well, however they are usually small in nature, although some successful firms such as Grameen Bank have managed to gain scale. Large companies need to be much more involved in this area, as entrepreneurs often have little access to capital and will need support in order to progress. Poverty exists on a large scale and thus the solutions must also be scalable.

Michael E Porter and Mark R Kramer explain that "real social entrepreneurship should be measured by its ability to create shared value, not just social benefit."[11] The concept of CSV recognizes that the needs of

[10] "HP and African Social Enterprise mPedigree Network Fight Counterfeit Drugs in Africa", 6 December 2010 www.hp.com/us/en/hp-news/press-release.html?id=814373#. UzAXxU1F3Dc

[11] Porter, Michael E. and Kramer, Mark R., "Creating Shared Value", *Harvard Business Review*, January 2011, http://hbr.org/2011/01/the-big-idea-creating-shared-value/

society really define markets and economies, and not conventional economic needs as per the Corporate Social Responsibility (CSR) approach. It focuses on the connection between societal and economic progress, thus suggesting that what is good for society is also good for firms and businesses in the economy.

There are different ways of implementing the CSV approach described in this article including the reconceiving of products and markets and redefining productivity in the value chain, but one of particular interest is, "enabling local cluster development."[12] Companies are not at all self-contained and their successes tend to be influenced by providing support for companies and the surrounding infrastructure. "Clusters" are geographic concentrations of related firms and providers, and are the main influence upon a firm's innovation, creation and productivity rates and levels. Some examples given in the article are IT in Silicon Valley, cut flowers in Kenya, and diamond cutting in Surat, India. The construction of these clusters help firms create shared value, as it improves the overall productivity and efficiency of the firm, while also considering and solving troubling areas and failures in the structure surrounding the cluster. Procurement benefits come from efficiency in the ability to obtain and develop the geographic concentrations.[13]

The paper also highlights that "a key aspect of cluster building in developing and developed countries alike is the formation of open and transparent markets."[14] This means that productivity is not at its full capacity when markets are inefficient or monopolized, due to unbalanced procedures and unfairness, such as the exploitation of workers. With open markets, the company is more able to get better deals with their suppliers, while also encouraging efficiency and better quality from them. In addition, workers can receive higher wages and the purchasing power of

---

[12] *Ibid.*

[13] *Ibid.*

[14] *Ibid.*

citizens will improve. This therefore "amplifies the connection between its success and its communities' success,"[15] and the growth results in multiplier effects: increasing jobs, new companies form and demand for subsidiary services rises."

A good example of achieving a positive CSV result through cluster development is Nestlé.

Nestlé has a comprehensive approach to CSV and has built clusters that have improved the efficiency of its new procurement practices. For example, the company built "agricultural, technical, financial, and logistical firms and capabilities in each coffee region to increase access to essential agricultural inputs such as plant stock, fertilizers, and irrigation equipment; strengthen regional farmer co-ops by helping them finance shared wet-milling facilities for producing higher-quality beans; and support an extension programme to advise all farmers on growing techniques."[16] All this provided benefits to Nestlé as well as the surrounding firms and companies in alliance with it.

The company has a well-articulated stance on CSV, affirming that it is the approach they take to the business as a whole in order to build a business capable of superior shareholder value, as well as helping people to improve their nutrition. They actively manage their commitments to "environmental, social and economic sustainability needed for operating our factories and for the sustainable growth and development of the communities and countries where we have operations. This involves substantial training and education of people inside and outside of Nestlé, as well as large investments in technology with lower environmental impact."[17] The company goes on to stipulate that CSV requires compliance with

---

[15] *Ibid.*

[16] *Ibid.*

[17] Nestlé S.A, Public Affairs, "Nestlé in Society", March 2014, http://storage.nestle.com/Interactive_CSV_2013/index.html#4/z

the highest standards of business practice, as well as their own code of Business Conduct, Corporate Business Principles, and Management and Leadership Principles.

The concept of shared value is good for both the public and private sectors. Who creates that value in what combinations does not really matter as long as society benefits. In all successful cases benefits are proven for all parties. Private sector companies tend to benefit from increases in productivity through the development of new business models and a demonstration of commitment to societal concerns, and public sector organizations from societal benefits that increase their standing and secure a better future for their communities.

NGO's are increasingly becoming major players in the creation of shared value. For example, TechnoServe has worked with companies to develop better agriculture in many countries, as has The Bill and Melinda Gates Foundation. Their objectivity and societal concern has helped bridge gaps between governments and industry and enhanced cooperation between them.

In an FSG article by Porter, Hills, Pfitzer, Patscheke and Hawkins, there is an absorbing detailed analysis of the measurement of shared value, and a good summary of the win-win situations that can be gained between the public and private sectors in terms of commercial and societal benefits.[18]

To summarize, the concept of Creating Shared Value takes the more commonly-known methods of CSR to a much more advanced stage where the whole of a business re-orientates itself for social (and commercial) benefit. This community-focused approach, where the private sector can build its brand equity and value, reward its stakeholders, and benefit society in equal measure, is indicative of the future of partnerships between public and private sector brands.

---

[18] Porter, Michael E. et al, "Measuring Shared Value",published by FSG
www.fsg.org/tabid/191/ArticleId/740/Default.aspx?srpush=true

Summary

This book has outlined the importance of branding to the public sector, from nations and industries to non-profit and other organizations. There are several drivers for the trend towards public sector branding, including the unending quest for tourists, investors, talent, membership, donations, and the export of goods and services. The underlying platform for these is the "dash for cash" in crowded and competitive markets, and the need for higher growth and standards of living for the increasingly large world population.

The development of brands that focus on the needs of various customer groups has been both successful and sustainable in the private sector, and the public sector is following suit, using the very same techniques. The benefits have been proven successful in the public sector to date and many countries and organizations are carrying out branding activities of one sort or another to achieve a multitude of objectives. These activities are not confined to developing countries but to developed countries as global barriers to trade and employment continue to be eroded; however emerging economies are perhaps in more desperate situations. Global changes and challenges dominate media headlines and need strategic responses. Branding is a formidable strategic response when implemented well.

The trend towards public sector branding will accelerate in the future and new forms of activity will emerge. Global partnerships and networks that focus on community-based operations and generate shared value while demonstrating corporate social responsibility will increase. Social enterprise will flourish, and sustainable and eco-friendly brands will become more visible. But only the most respected and trusted of these will become the great brands of the future, as the world over people search for ethical solutions to personal and organizational challenges.

The speed of change will increase; faster will be better; flexibility and adaptability are factors that will flourish; and innovation will be a "must have" not a "nice to have." And these activities will need to engage both the private and public sectors. Growth depends on innovation, the generation and adoption of new knowledge and ideas. Often governments do not have the financial resources that businesses need to innovate and grow. New questions in every country will be asked such as how social investment can be fostered, and how fast the public service can be changed. And given that over 50 per cent of the world's research and development is now in the hands of around 700 private sector companies, what needs to be done so that this can be shared with the public sector to make a stronger social impact. Some organizations are now grappling with these issues, such as Nesta (formerly NESTA, National Endowment for Science, Technology and the Arts), an independent charity that works to increase the innovation capacity of the UK and has a mission to "help people and organizations bring great ideas to life."[19]

There is no doubt at all that branding will continue to grow in the public sector as more countries and public sector organizations seek to gain an advantage that will cut through cluttered markets and build their identity and image. In the future, the public sector will become more sophisticated in its use of branding techniques. There will be a greater use of social media to conduct conversations with different target audiences and there will be a movement towards tracking brand success not just by measuring brand equity but also by measuring brand value. Organizations involved in both developed and developing countries will engage more in branding activity, but emerging markets and developing countries will indulge in it to a greater extent. The focus on branding and transforming the public service of countries will become more acute as countries strive to achieve greater competitiveness.

Indeed, one of the great challenges of this century will be to discover how public sector leaders can contribute to, and build, innovative organizations and nations which serve the needs of developed and developing economies and communities. This will not be achieved by looking solely

---

[19] www.nesta.org.uk/

at improving the tangible aspects of innovative businesses such as operations, systems, technology, research and development and products and services, but also by building powerful brands that link closely to public sector objectives and strategies and put customers at the forefront of everything they do in order to keep moving forward.

No country or public sector organization can avoid the need to constantly transform and change, and this is perhaps the strategic competitive advantage that branding techniques bring to the public sector. Branding is really concerned with the perpetual management of change for the benefit of all customers and communities.

Finally, it is important to emphasize that the building of successful public sector brands in the future will demand not just on-going transformational change but also the development of a strong internal brand culture and stakeholder mind set. Politicians will need to assess and enhance the impact of their policies on nation brands in order to grow their economies; public services will need to be faster, more flexible, and provide customer experiences that can rival the best of the private sector; and all public sector organizations, including NGOs, will need to use brand more strategically as a competitive weapon in an age where a strong brand image brings with it significant attraction, power, and value.

AUTHOR BIOGRAPHY

Dr Paul Temporal is a leading global expert on brand strategy and management, whose main interests lie in the fields of national and corporate branding. He has over 25 years of experience in brand consulting and training, having consulted for many governments and top corporations around the world, and is well known for his practical and results-oriented approach. Paul is an Associate Fellow at both Saïd Business School and Green Templeton College in the University of Oxford, and a Visiting Professor in Marketing at Shanghai Jiao Tong University, China.

Aside from working with some of the world's top private sector brands, there are public sector organizations to which he has also been a consultant. These include APEC, ASEAN, OIC, UNCTAD, and the Governments of Brunei, Canada, China, Dubai, Hong Kong, Malaysia, Oman, New Zealand, Singapore, Thailand, United Arab Emirates, and the United Kingdom. He has also worked with many ministries, departments, statutory bodies and GLCs in these countries. In addition, he has worked with the UK Civil Service, World Bank, European Union, and three African governments.

Paul is a much sought-after speaker and has been a regular contributor at major international conferences and round-table events, such as those organized by The Economist Group, *Business Week* and World Islamic Economic Forum.

Paul has also published widely in many journals and media and has featured in mainstream global media such as *The New York Times, The Wall Street Journal, Sunday Times of India,* and CNBC. He has written numerous bestselling books, including *Branding in Asia, Romancing the Customer, Asia's Star Brands, Advanced Brand Management (second edition),* and *Islamic Branding and Marketing.*

ACKNOWLEDGEMENTS

In writing this book I have been given ideas and assistance from many colleagues, professionals, and organizations from the public sector. I would, however, like especially to thank the following people.

Firstly, I would like to thank Professor Philip Kotler and Miles Young for their friendship, advice, inspiration and encouragement over many years and during the writing of this book.

I would also like to give thanks to the following people and organizations that have assisted me with many of the cases in this book. They include the Ministry of Primary Resources and Industry, Brunei Darussalam, and the Brunei Halal Industry Innovation Centre team; Lucy Donlan and Tourism Australia; Wee Ping Tan and WWF International; Richard Bridger and Populus Limited; and David Haigh, Tom Connell, Bryn Anderson and the team at Brand Finance plc.

I would also like to thank my colleagues at Saïd Business School, University of Oxford, as well as Maria Temporal for her valuable assistance in editing the manuscript.

Finally, my gratitude extends to all at John Wiley & Sons who continue to give me great support, and have been so helpful in the development, production and marketing of this book.

INDEX